The Unknown Woman Within

Creating the Love Affair with You

Torre M. Prothro, M.A.

iUniverse, Inc.
New York   Bloomington

The Unknown Woman Within
Creating the Love Affair with You

iUniverse books may be ordered through booksellers or by contacting:

iUniverse
1663 Liberty Drive
Bloomington, IN 47403
www.iuniverse.com
1-800-Authors (1-800-288-4677)

ISBN: 978-1-4401-5567-3 (pbk)
ISBN: 978-1-4401-5569-7 (cloth)
ISBN: 978-1-4401-5568-0 (ebk)

Printed in the United States of America

iUniverse rev. date: 7/23/2009

To the memories of my grandmother Effie Mae Holt and my best friend Tosha Tiyette Taylor. I know that each day you two are looking down over me with your amazing smiling faces, and I know that you know that each and every day I miss you and reach out to you. My life is so much better in so many ways because I had the opportunity to share some of it with you. I will see you both on the other side. God bless, I love you.

Acknowledgments

I would like to thank my family and friends for their support and love during the terrifying times of my divorce and throughout the making of this book. If it is true that true wealth is having wonderful family and friends, I am a very wealthy lady. I continuously thank God for how blessed and rich I am for sharing my life with you all.

To the women in my life: **Marsha Holt**, my mother and my best friend, thank you for constantly pushing me to be the best that I can be. You have been here for me when I could not be here for myself. I love you with all my heart and I thank you for never giving up on me and my dreams even when I had. **Alarie Prothro**, a good friend who has shown me in so many ways the love and tenderness women should have for their families. Thank you for loving me as your daughter. I love you. **Kennedy Prothro,** my niece, thanks for all your love and support. **Hailey and Jordan Hood**, my children, my loves, and my futures, you two have no idea how you have changed my life, inspired me to create new dreams, and given me the determination to see these dreams through. Mommie loves you and thanks God each day for the unconditional love and insurmountable joy that you two bring to my life. **Victoria Wiley**, the newest edition to my family, you are my daughter and, I am sure, my future friend. I love you as my very own.

To the men in my life: **George W. Prothro Sr.,** my father and my friend. Daddy, thank you for teaching me how a real man looks, behaves, and loves. You have been an excellent example of what a man is. I love you with all my heart. **George W. Prothro Jr.,** my brother, thank you for all of the laughter, talks, fights, prayers, hugs, and pats on the back. You and I have been through a lifetime of changes, and I am proud to say you are my friend who just happens to be my big brother. I love you. **Jonathan, Kyle, Marcus, and Mikele Holt,** my baby brothers, thank you for your love and support. I love you guys. **James Thomas Wiley Jr.,** my husband, my love and my confidant, from the moment you entered my life you have made it easier, sweeter, and more exciting. Thank you for showing me love in the unselfish and courageous way that you do.

To my friends: Dr. Tracy Smith, Pamela Thomas, Shelia Stancil, Angela Bell, Angela White, Dazara Ware, Shelia Ford, Carol Veneables, Wyomme Grubbs, Claudia Milsap, Sheresa Melvin, Maureen Cahill, Kathan Fillingim, Sophie Mengistu, Jermaine Warren, and Michael McCrae. You guys have been in my life through many different seasons, but one thing you all have in common is listening, encouraging, and sharing my dreams with me. Thank you for all of the laughs, tears, advice, and prayers. I love you all like sisters and brothers. A special thank-you to Francis Mossynski for your technical support and awesome web designs. You all have been such a tremendous help to me. I hope you know that if I can ever be of service or support, I am always here for you.

In closing, I want to thank my Lord and savior, Jesus Christ, for keeping me and holding me up during the storms, struggles, and disappointing moments of my life. I hope that through your grace and love I may be able to touch and help others. Thank you for your mercy. I love you. Amen.

Contents

Introduction

An unfortunate but frequent situation that arises while being in love is not knowing how to love or how to receive love. We spend a great deal of time contemplating or daydreaming about falling in love and having a happily-ever-after story. Many of us never realize that in order to have this great love story, we must first have the appropriate tools to ensure us of success in love. A big mistake that we as women make is not falling *first* in love with ourselves.

The thought of not having a story of our own about some great man in our lives frightens most of us and forces us to move too quickly, rushing into what we think is love. Sadly, what most of us fail to realize is that what happens to us before, during, and after the breakup of a painful relationship is more likely than the happily-ever-after story. We live our lives hoping for a Prince Charming or a Mr. Right to come and take us away from it all, but in reality, we never had the tools or knowledge of how to love *ourselves*, let alone anyone else.

Women usually do what needs to be done in almost all other facets of our lives. We go to school, get a good job, learn to make a decent living for ourselves, and yet we are still searching for someone else to make things happen for us inside of this love game that we play out in our minds. We continually focus, no matter how good our current situation is, on getting that happily-ever-after story. The happily-ever-after story is supposed to link us to being whole and complete.

Well, in the real world, the relationships between men and women are constantly evolving. Times have changed, and so have the games between men and women. Whatever happened to men knowing how and when to romance a girl? Whatever happened to a woman knowing her opponent (mate) so well she would have him eating out of the palm of her hand? These questions perplex many of us. We are still looking for Mr. Yesterday instead of Mr. Tomorrow.

No matter how much education we achieve or money we earn, women are still looking for *the man*—the one who will make life easier, sweeter, and more alive than ever. Oftentimes, this man has come. However, we were so blinded by what society says we should seek in a man; we just could not see him. We find ourselves in a perpetual state of looking and searching for him based on previous failed relationships and on what others believe to be an ideal mate for us.

We very rarely stop and reassess our positions, needs, wants, or disappointments. We are in pursuit of the next candidate to fill an empty whole that only we ourselves can truly fill. What happens to us before, during, and throughout love is not the only precursor to the next relationship. It all begins well before the first love or first real relationship starts. It all begins with you.

It took me a while to realize this concept in my own life. I looked for approval, validation, love, and yes, pleasure from my mate. My life was centered around my mate's mood, attitude, needs, achievements, failures, and dysfunctions. His path in life was more interesting and important than my own.

Now, how in the world did all this happen? It happened to me like to most other women—I was dreaming of the happily-ever-after story.

I was not focused on my future with or without a man. I was

focused on his life and it being the majority of mine. It happened because I allowed it to.

I turned over my life in the hope that he would give me a part of his. In my mind, it was okay to give one hundred percent of me to someone who was only offering a portion of himself to me. Luckily, I realized I needed and deserved more from my mate and from myself. I had to make some serious changes in my life. So you see, ladies, if you are going through similar turmoil or battles, you are not alone. We all have these problems, and we all at some time or another need to make changes in our lives.

The purpose of this book is to encourage and assist women who are struggling in a tumultuous relationship with their mates and themselves. It is meant to provide knowledge and kinship to women who are fearful and shaken by their current situation but ready to venture into something new. When we are not at peace or in harmony within, we will in many instances choose a diversion or a mate that reflects the pain or struggle within us.

My hope is that this book will reach women and encourage them while they make the harsh decisions that all too often come with living and loving. I hope this book makes the journey a little more tolerable. While going through any adversity or struggle, there are a few variables that we as women need to perfect in order to be successful with our endeavors. This book, I hope, will illustrate to you that each and every one of us already possesses these variables within. Further, it will also explain to you how to discover them and how to effectively utilize them in your everyday living.

Every girl needs to possess a certain few necessary components before the "big search" for Mr. Right should even begin. These components will enable her to be confident, peaceful, and patient while playing the dating and relationship games that are all out there waiting for her. They will provide her with the blueprints she will need to, first, find her true potential and then, hopefully, find her mate. These vital pieces will restructure her in such a way that she will overcome her fears, her pains, her mistakes, and, yes, her past. We all suffer from pain in our past and the misguided unfortunate mistakes that we have made. However, playing the victim role or lying down and not getting back up are in no way the answer or the next strategic move to make.

The key ingredients or variables needed to aid you in the pursuit of your *Unknown Woman* are Power, Strength, Forgiveness, and Knowledge and Wisdom. We all have an unknown woman deep down inside, and she is dying to be discovered and activated within us. Are you ready to heal yourself and try life with her in the driver's seat? Well, if you are thinking or feeling *yes* in answer to this question, hold on and believe that she will be found by the one and only person who can. That person, of course, is you.

POWER

"That a woman can change herself ... and master
her own destiny is the conclusion of every mind who
is wide-awake to the power of right thought."

—Christian D. Larson (1874-1954)

There are so many ways in which our society depicts power. We have all been fooled to believe that power is obtained by being famous, or having an abundance of money. The media perpetuates these ideas by constantly showing us images of beautiful, rich, and successful women. We hardly, if ever see real power. True power is loving yourself no matter where you are in life. It is shown by the love we have for ourselves that transfers to others. True power is having integrity, strength, and the determination to weather whatever life has in store for us. Power is a necessity and a tool needed to obtain your Unknown Woman Within.

Chapter 1
The Power of a Woman

If we are really honest with ourselves, we must admit that many of our pains and frustrations begin from within. As women, we have such an innate component within us to self-hate and abuse ourselves. Now I am not equipped to understand what it is to be born male, and I sure as heck do not know how to live as one; however, what I know for sure is that being raised female is a painstaking, emotional, heart-wrenching, and glorious experience.

We learn very early on that we are viewed differently and expected to behave differently than men. There is something so special and intrinsically unique about being born to the female species. We know we are the bearers of life, and yet most of us find nothing beautiful or sacred about ourselves. We know we give balance and stability to our homes, and yet most of us feel unappreciated and of no value to anyone. We do possess brains and in most cases are very intelligent, but many of us resort to playing or portraying dumb in order to make others feel more important and comfortable around us. In almost all phases of any woman's life, you will find some form of insecurity, fear, or inferiority.

We are all too often overwhelmed and taken over by these emotions. This is not to say that it is wrong to feel these human emotions from time to time. However, they should not consume, control, or be a major foundation of our existence in supposed loving relationships. Women have had to establish their role and power since the very beginning of time.

In the Garden of Eden, Eve (the first woman on earth) convinced Adam (the first man on earth), who had a direct physical, mental, and emotional connection with God, to eat the forbidden fruit that God himself had forbidden him to eat. Now, ladies, this must have been one heck of a woman to be able to sway Adam from his maker's orders. We are awesome and splendid creatures. We are awesome because God made us to be smart, beautiful, and yes, powerful.

What Eve did was wrong, but she was given some kind of gift or talent to make Adam listen to her and give into her. If we learn to accept and surrender to these special gifts that God has given us for the good and not for the bad, just think of how powerful we could be.

Throughout centuries, we have been able to develop dynasties and kingdoms through these talents. Women in the past had nowhere near the power, freedom, or education that we do today. However, such women as Cleopatra, Queen Elizabeth, Joan of Arc, and Marie Antoinette were all able to accomplish what most of us today have absolutely no clue of how to even begin. This is not some old mystery or secret.

These women believed in themselves and used the times and the knowledge that they had to get the job done. So why is it that today we live in a world where we are reduced to being sexy, stupid, or fearful and being preyed upon by others? We are still competing with one another based on our beauty, marital status, and whether or not we have children. This is a very unfortunate place to still be in since there has been so much other progress within our society for women.

This lack of self-assurance and peace within the female experience should be put in the proper perspective and then left there. It should never again be the vehicle that many of us drive through our lives in.

Times are changing, and there is no longer a need or place for insecure, fearful, and desperate women. We are still in constant and perpetual unawareness of our strength, potential, and destinies *if* we allow others to determine when and where our happiness will exist. *We* need to be at peace within ourselves. This peace is paramount for us to possess in order to live the full and productive lives we are hopefully striving for.

Have you ever noticed how men stick together and back each other up in times of trouble; even if they are in competition with each other? They seem to have this secret underground boys' club that keeps them unified and together in many circumstances. We, on the other hand and in most instances, will drop a girlfriend, a dream, and/or a family member in a second for the hope of a man's attention or approval. There seems to be no loyalty among women. We can be so catty and underhanded in our everyday dealings with each other. Society has been able to place so many burdens on women that we seem ready to do nowadays whatever is necessary to get a man and to hold onto him.

What happened to the power of simply knowing ourselves? When women were not allowed to work, they still possessed an assuredness of self. The women of our grandmothers' day did not have the freedom that we do, but they had so much more sense of self and what their contribution was to their families and communities. Where is the confidence we once had? Where is the assurance that one day we will have what we so rightfully deserve? This confidence was the foundation that created and guided the feminist movement.

Women of the past were not afraid of never finding Mr. Right. They made it in life with or without him. Where is the strength in believing, come hell or high water, that if he does not come, I will make it on my own? I will not only make it on my own, but I will be happy while I wait, and I will enjoy the life God has given to me. Why do we still insist on determining whether or not we are whole by the status of being married or single? This is an awareness that needs to be conveyed to our younger women so we will stop promoting scared and insecure women.

Ladies, I hope most of us realize that strong women produce strong communities and that weak and fearful women produce weak and preyed upon communities. If you think I am wrong, just look at our communities right now. The communities our grandmothers fostered were stronger, more productive, and much more unified than ours. No matter what emotional state we are in, we contribute that same state of being to our homes and our communities. What picture of power are we projecting to our families and society as a whole?

> *"Do not fear your inner thoughts, opinions, or power!*
> *We do know what is best for us! Just trust yourself!"*
> —Constance Bryant

Marsha, a young divorced mother with three kids, lives in an urban inner city and is struggling to make ends meet. She is in her second year of pursuing her Bachelor's degree in business, and Marsha is tired of hustling and being without a broad shoulder to rest upon at night. She is lonely and, most of all, tired of making it happen all on her own. Marsha is a beautiful woman and is propositioned all the time from different men at her waitressing job if she would go out with them.

Marsha is no fool, and she knows what dating these men would involve. She remembers hearing her mother telling her to stay close to God and to remain on her journey. "If you lay down with dogs, you will get up with fleas, Marsha." That was one of her favorite lines to keep Marsha straight.

Well, one day, she is approached by a very rich, attractive, and powerful man who tells her he is unhappily married and would love to help her out with her financial problems as well as her kids. The rent is due, and Marsha is tired of struggling—but deep down inside, she knows that once she agrees to lower herself to this so-called proposition, she would then be no different than the lowlife that offered her this so-called great deal.

Marsha focuses on the fact that in two years she will have her college degree in business and will certainly be in a better position. She then very graciously declines his offer. This was a hard decision for her at this time in her life. However, after thinking it over, a sense of esteem and pride fills her soul.

Life is filled with these types of situations for us as women. In order for us to make a difference, we have to begin from within. Marsha could have accepted his offer and allowed her kids to see how she compromised herself and them for a few dollars. What would her daughters get from that silent message? What would her son get from that silent message? What would Marsha stoop to next after this offer has run its course or is no longer enough for her? See, we as women affect so many others with the decisions and manners in which we conduct ourselves. What could have happened to that man's wife and his children had the affair become public knowledge? This one bad decision could cause many others pain in the years to come.

"No matter what you do, always do what you know to be right." These words I grew up listening to time after time after time. It has not always been easy to follow, and there have been times that I did not do what was right—and, yes, I paid for it. Being strong and powerful means making the right decisions even when we don't want to.

It is funny how what a person hears over and over again becomes a part of them—it sticks. If you are told that you are stupid, ugly, and fat, you believe that immediately. However, hearing good things about yourself, for many of us, takes a lot more time to grab hold of us. Luckily, the saying is true that practice does make perfect.

Try to start programming yourself to do what you know to be right, even if it is difficult to do. Start telling yourself every day all day what you would like to be. Begin by telling yourself you are strong, powerful, courageous, beautiful, smart, God-fearing, and whatever else positive it is you secretly wish to be down within your soul. It is almost as if we come into this world prepared for the pain and anguish of living, rather than the joy and success of living. We are in many situations programmed to be unhappy. So, let's try to reverse this program. Begin each day reversing your past ill-willed thoughts and actions by thinking positively and confidently about you.

How does a woman become powerful? How powerful would you like to become? Are you afraid of being strong and powerful? These are questions that hopefully you are asking yourself or would like to know the answers to. A woman's financial status, education, or skills in manipulation have nothing to do with her power. A woman's power is in direct accordance with her integrity, love of self, and love of others. Once a woman has full awareness of who she is and what her purpose is in life, she can begin to understand how and what she can contribute to her community and to others. Power is when a woman knows how to change herself in order to change others.

In the above example, Marsha had a choice to make regarding her integrity. If she had chosen poorly, she could have hurt and affected many others by her decision. The choice that she made was not an easy one to make, but it allowed her to sleep at night knowing that she—and no one else—was still in control of her and her family's future. Marsha made a powerful stand for herself, and she more than likely earned the respect of the man who had propositioned her.

No one respects a weak, unaware person, especially not a powerful, successful man. There are many women who would relinquish their power and respect over to a man for the unsure notion of financial security and a life a little easier than what they are normally accustomed to. However, Marsha decided to invest in herself and her current agenda to better her living situation. Marsha took a step toward self-empowerment.

She chose to believe in herself and not live in a fairy-tale world of Mr. Right or Mr. Right Now to see her through a rough spot. These so-called rough spots in life are where we learn to stand and fight for what is ours and what we believe in. Power can start with just the simple decision to be totally and completely independent and free from others' influences over your life.

What does power look and feel like? It looks like being in control of your life. It looks like knowing that no matter what, you are special and important regardless of your financial status or the size dress you wear. Power is a reflection of who you are inside. It is a reflection of every decision that you have made in your life. If we were to take a look at the lives of Oprah Winfrey, Condoleezza Rice, Tyra Banks, or Hillary Rodham Clinton, we would see the many decisions they have made, but we would also see the reverence and fearlessness that comes with being powerful, successful, and confident women.

Most successful women are placed in compromising situations one after another, and in most of them they choose to make the right decision. There were probably many poor choices made as well, but what a powerful woman does is to make a right from her wrong and continue to pursue her dreams and aspirations. She does not blame another for her wrong decisions, nor does she play the victim and throw her hands up in desperation and defeat.

Powerful women are representations of the choices that they have made, both good and bad. They are no different than you. *They only chose differently than you did.* Your choice is your road to your future.

If you want a successful and happy future, you must make the right choices.

You have to discipline yourself to make better decisions for your life. A successful woman is okay with, and in many circumstances comfortable with, sacrificing the right now for the future. She has disciplined herself in such a way that settling for anything less than what she aspires to is simply not enough. A successful woman knows that she must take responsibility for her accomplishments as well as her mistakes.

The successful women of the world get up and move on from their mistakes. They do not wallow in their misguided decisions. They use poor decisions and bad mistakes as tools to discipline and refine themselves. They do not mind sacrificing and waiting to get what is rightfully theirs, whether it be careers, men, children, fame, and/or success. So, ladies, get up and get going and know that your happiness, success, and yes, your power all begin within you. Find peace and power by living in a constant state of integrity, love, and discipline.

RECAP OF CHAPTER 1

1. Stop being afraid of your power and potential.
2. The journey to finding your power is a constant and enduring process.
3. The power of a woman is congruent with her integrity, responsibility, and commitment to others.
4. Learning from your personal mistakes and bad decisions is all part of the journey toward finding your power.
5. Powerful women are a representation of the choices that they have made, both good and bad.

Chapter 2
To Thy Self Be True

Growing up female in this country means many different things. We were once told we are not as strong, intelligent, or dynamic as men. A boy child is still viewed in many homes and families as being superior and more of a blessing than a girl child. Growing up female has also been congruent as being a liability for many families. The paternal name will die off if a boy child is not born (and, of course, often the mother is blamed if a boy child is not birthed).

This whole fallacy was, of course, digested and accepted by many of us. In order to keep it a predominately man's world, there has to be an oppressed woman, a woman who has to answer to a man in all parameters of her life. This means in order for her to fit properly into a man's world, she must first know her place and then, of course, stay in it as well. It has only been forty years since women have been allowed to express themselves freely without a lot of opposition and strife. This is all stated to prove that we are now a different breed of women, and it also means we expect to be treated differently as well.

"Power is knowing what works and what
does not work for you anymore."
—Wyomme Grubbs

Trying to live up to expectations of the past will not work. We have changed, and they have changed. We can no longer expect the same things from men while we insist upon being treated differently in corporate offices, in sports arenas, and in the bedroom. At some point, we are going to have to deal with the fact that in our own changing, we have changed others as well.

We have changed the entire dating process. Men no longer know how to approach us because of all of the change within us. We are living a man's lifestyle but still seeking to be taken care of by a man in the same manner as our mothers and grandmothers were. We need to wake up, Sleeping Beauties, and embrace this change we have fought for. How can we honestly expect men to respect our newfound independence and yet still want to treat us like the women of our past?

David meets Erin in college, and they begin to discuss their plans for the future. They agree that both of them should stick with their own plans while dating each other. However, as time progresses, the young girl is spending more time on him and less time focused on her own pursuits. The young man pursues her; however, he still remains zoned in on his main target, his future.

He tries to keep her happy in the relationship, but his main attention is given to his future. He will not compromise at all in regards to this matter and has told Erin so. Erin has forgotten who she is and what she wants. How can she expect David to respect and value her dreams when she has so quickly forgotten them?

Ladies, we should be so self-assured and confident in our dreams and future that we are not swayed by our emotions and feelings. There is nothing we cannot do once we put our minds to it. Today we are doctors, lawyers, politicians, producers, and directors, and yet we are still under the siege of loving and being loved by a man. Making mistakes in love has cost us all too much time, money, and above all heartache. In order for us to better position ourselves in the matters of self-love, we need to make a few adjustments.

How can we effectively love a man when we are not honest in knowing who we are? Many of us fall in love for the first time at a young age. Now tell me, how many of us are anywhere close to being the same person that we were at fifteen or sixteen years old? We are in a completely different mind-set, financial status, and emotional state than what we were at sixteen years of age. Being true to who you are takes time and life lessons, but hopefully we can learn from others' mistakes and begin to learn a little sooner than most of us have in the past.

Hopefully this lesson in life will reach some of the younger readers and restrain them from making some of the mistakes that many of us older women have made. Learning to trust your inner voices and being honest with yourself is one of the first steps to make in being true to thy self. You must release the fear of who you are and stand firmly inside of yourself regardless of what life is presenting to you.

Why is it that most of us do not hear, let alone listen, to ourselves, mothers, grandmothers, or girlfriends until the damage is already done? Unfortunately for some strange reason, we have to be pregnant, have our credit screwed up, or—God forbid—be already diagnosed with an STD before we take heed to already damn good advice.

This is the area that we will focus on next, ladies. Whenever we are in a relationship that we know is unfulfilling or just plain wrong for us, why do we make excuses for the screwed-up relationship and try to fool our loved ones, or more importantly ourselves? We usually do not respond or pay attention to the voices within or the good advice from our loved ones.

Honesty is the best policy for almost any situation; however, it is even more important when you're dealing with yourself. If you are not honest with yourself, how can you really know what you want and how to get what you want from yourself and others? There is no way of being happy if you are not first and foremost honest with yourself. I have seen it time and time again in myself and in my relationships with others. I could not see myself being happy or at peace because I could not be honest with my inner voices.

My stomach and my soul were screaming at me to move on, get out, and/or leave the unhealthy relationship, but instead, I did what I thought was safe. I stayed. Many people (friends and family members) told me to wait and not marry when I did. I was so in love and afraid to be without my ex-husband that I kept on pushing him to marry me. Deep in the pit of my being, I knew it was not right, but I was determined to make it right and live the happily-ever-after story.

My biggest fear at that time in my life was to be the girl who dated a guy for a long time and he never married her. I seldom thought about what I wanted for my future or for myself; I just focused on being married. Now when I look back at that young girl, I am saddened that I could not see life as satisfying or fulfilling without being married. My one and only agenda was to get married.

Whether he was right or wrong for me was trivial. I had to have a man commit himself to me for life in order for me to feel loved and acceptable. Now I know this all seems ridiculous, but trust me, it was very hard for me to admit it was true. Happiness for me at that time was first and foremost being married. There was no other option.

My hope for any of you reading this with this same affliction is that you will be calm and assured that peace within is obtainable, and that you will know that you can fall in love with your life right now no matter what it lacks or possesses because it is the only life you've got. It does not matter if you have that great guy, job, or lifestyle. Your life is important right now in the midst of whatever you have created for yourself, good or bad. You make the choices, so fix what needs to be fixed and start by being honest with yourself until you know what your next move is going to be.

> *"Listen to your inner voice and trust it."*
> —Angela Bell

April earns six figures a year and is in her late thirties. She has recently married and has no children. She now realizes she wants children, but her husband is not on board just yet. He is still in school and not ready to take on the additional expenses of a baby.

April feels all of her accomplishments are now secondary, allowing self-doubt and the voice of society to control her once-happy existence. Many of her friends and family are telling her she has to stay home with a new baby and that her husband would have to be the primary breadwinner for it all to work out.

Her everyday worries are all intermingled with the dreams of getting pregnant and being a stay-at-home mother. The one thing she said she would never do is now the one thing keeping her away from true happiness. April is now listening to what others have to say about her future happiness. Why would she allow her happiness to be entangled in what others say is right for her?

The one thing most men know and utilize from being boys is that they have to take care of themselves and their families. Women are still new to earning large sums of money and having financial freedom; however, we are not new to raising families all on our own.

We know how to be mothers, sisters, daughters, wives, and anything else presented to us by our lives.

In the above example, April is successful, independent, and quickly becoming unhappy. She has made something of herself in spite of her gender, and yet a major void is left in her life. She is allowing what others think and say to stifle her current goals and future agenda.

Ladies, we need to realize we are living a different life than our grandmothers and we are now in a man's space. The time has come for us to redefine how, when, and where our future will take us. To the many women with this particular problem, please find peace and solace in the knowledge that if you could overcome all of those other obstacles in life, then you can overcome this one as well. No matter how your situation ends up, know that you are the most important player inside your play. It will work out and however it works out, life is too short to spend it unhappy and disappointed.

Why worry about who will be home with the baby or who is the breadwinner? April makes enough money to be the primary breadwinner. Her future is not as dim as others may preach it to be. All she needs to do is first make plans with her husband about their possible future family and then take action as she has always done in her past endeavors.

We have to see things realistically and practically. Making the decision to be a professional career woman and mother may be difficult, but April is an intelligent and accomplished person—she can figure it out. Most men know what they want and how they are going to get it. They have studied what is necessary to win, and they take hold of it with both hands. We have to be just as realistic and dedicated to our current situation and dreams in order to make it happen for us as well. We cannot have it all, but we can come very close.

If we can learn to first be honest with ourselves, then we should be able to see things a little more clearly. In the next example, a young woman is in denial about her current relationship and how to obtain what she is seeking in life. Honesty is definitely the first step she needs to take in order to attain her future aspirations. If she can learn to be honest with herself, she may find the courage to remove the fear that is leading her to denial.

Karen has been in a relationship with Keith for four years, and from the very beginning of the courtship, she has told him of her desires to have children and to have her own family. From the very start of the courtship, Keith has said that he did not want to marry and start a family. Karen still continues to believe that she can obtain her initial goals with Keith.

Throughout the four-year relationship, the primary argument has been when will they get engaged and begin to settle down. Keith is surprised at how Karen has ignored his dreams for his life. Deep down, Karen truly believes that she can change his mind and get her needs meet.

This is a primary example of the need to be true to thy self. Why in the world would a woman give four years of her life to a man who has clearly stated from the start that he does not have the same vision or goals that she has? I will tell you why: *fear.*

She fears that her life is not special enough to make her happy. She fears that she will be alone. She fears that her dreams will not be fulfilled. She fears that she could possibly one day be happy, so she sabotages herself and remains with a man who does not want what she wants. All of these fears control her decisions and affect her everyday judgments.

Most human beings have a tendency to believe that they do not deserve to have their dreams met. I do not know why that is, but it is very true. Many of us enjoy being disappointed and controlled by other people. Why do we do this to ourselves? There are some of us who are fearful of being successful, so we live in a state of constant denial. We would rather be disappointed than to go out there and find real happiness.

Many of us are too *lazy and scared* to attempt to find real happiness. We would much rather complain and blame others for our losses instead of regrouping and sacrificing for a successful future. Life is a sequence of decisions and accomplishments, and in between them are several mistakes.

When the mistakes occur, we (successful women) tend to regroup and move forward, if we are lucky. However, there are many of us who fall down and cannot get back up. We lay there and become comfortable with the disappointment and pain. The underlying thoughts are "Well, I know what to expect from this, so I might as well stay with this mess instead of making a new mistake for myself."

Why would a woman remain in a relationship she knows cannot yield the ending she is seeking? She probably thinks to herself, "Why start over now? I do have companionship, extra money, and good sex. I know he will come around." Well, sweetheart, "News flash: he will not.*" If there is one thing I really want to convey to women in regard to this situation, it is that a man hardly if ever changes his mind or position about his future with you.

If a man says he does not wish to marry you, then you had better start to look for the next man to come along. Men typically place women in a category, and that category is usually where she will stay. If a man says you are for his pleasure and that is all, then honey, you are just for that and that is all.

Men know us a lot better than we know them. They know if you are the marrying kind, the screwing kind, or the friend kind. *So my question to you is, "What kind are you?"* I hope you are learning to be an honest and fearless woman so you can remove the mistakes you have made in the past and make a fresh new start.

Once you learn to be honest with yourself and remove your fear of success and happiness from the picture, what do you envision for yourself? Do you have any idea of what you want and how you will go about getting it? We ladies know how to look pretty, spend lots of money, and yes, even appear to be interested in what a man is saying most of the time. How many of us under the age of forty really know what we are truly made of? Do you possess the basic fundamentals of a successful woman—integrity, self-love, confidence, ambition, religion, compassion, motivation, passion, and joy for living?

It is similar and yet different for most of us. I thought I knew what I wanted and needed from life, but it was not until my early thirties that I really began to see myself in a definitive state. Once I was honest with myself and not afraid of working toward being happy, I realized I had no real imagination when it came to my full potential or destiny.

Now this is not to say that all of us are clueless when it comes to being completely self-aware, but it is true that the average, woman, spends more time on others than on herself.

Most people are embarrassed to say they do not know what they want or expect from life. It is almost a hidden rule among adults not to admit that you do not know what you want or how you will go about trying to achieve that certain something. Well, it is time to dispel this problem and teach ourselves to be true to our own selves.

> *"Power is believing in your decisions to be the one genuine person you were made to be."*
> —**Shelia Stancil**

FIRST THINGS FIRST

In order to find what you're looking for, it is usually best to *know* what you do not want. Most of us *think* we know what we want in life, but many times we simply don't. Why are we still in the dark when it comes to finding out what makes us tick? Why is it so difficult to figure out what is good to us and for us?

Wanting love is not as simple as we tend to think it is. Wanting the perfect man is, of course, *one* of our goals in life, but are *you* perfect for that future man? We spend so much time on them and finding them instead of finding ourselves. What do we need in order to be whole and ready for that perfect man when he does come? How will we know when we are really ready for the perfect man?

There are several variables that need to be in place for us to be knowledgeable about who we are. What were your dreams as a child? What brings you pleasure outside of a man? What hobbies do you possess without the presence of a man? Who do you run to or seek advice from in your times of need? What are your finances like now and for the next five, ten, twenty years?

These are some of the questions we should be asking and resolving on a daily basis. In order to know yourself, there has to be a place within you that only you can listen to and reason with. If we spend time alone and learn to listen to that voice within our heads, then we will be able to at least get to first base. How do we listen to ourselves? Our bodies always tell us our own personal truths, but for some strange reason, especially in our youth, we are not tuned-in from within to know how to listen to ourselves.

In the next example, a young woman is trying to figure out what her next move is. She is excited about her new accomplishment, but she is emotionally attached to something she really needs to put in check. There are many signs around her, and yet she still is unable to hear her inner voice.

Janie, a twenty-five-year-old woman, is finishing up college and trying to decide where to look for her first real job. A very exciting time for her, but she has a major issue in regard to the location of her possible new job.

21

Janie wants to live close to her boyfriend of three years, but the job that is offering the best starting position is a five-hour drive from her boyfriend.

Everyone near and dear to her has urged her to take the job and date her boyfriend from afar. Janie often dreams about her new position and how much better off her life would be once she begins this job. Deep down inside of her, she knows that she should take this great opportunity; however, their relationship has been rocky for a while, and she feels that being so far apart will only make matters worse. What should she do?

What would you do? I hope your answer is to take the job and date him from afar.

Why do we compromise ourselves for what we think is love? In most cases, if the role were reversed, Janie's boyfriend would not be making a compromise. A woman can be anything she puts her mind to, but for some strange reason, when it comes to matters of the heart, she is stupid as hell. That's right, I said stupid as hell. We will spend our whole lives preparing for a career or educating ourselves, and yet we make some of the most idiotic decisions in regard to what we think is love.

If a relationship is already rocky, maybe space is the thing needed here. If Janie has been seeing this man for three years and she is not sure what to expect from him, shouldn't she know what to expect from herself? Why should her future be delayed or put off because of a shaky relationship? If Janie was engaged and had a beautiful relationship with this man from the onset, then maybe she could seek other positions or options. However, it is an unhealthy and rocky romance, so why bother?

Most men would not even give it a second thought. Their careers come first, and they are all too quick to explain to us what is important and what comes first in their lives. Janie has been preparing for this her whole life, and yet she is willing to put all of her pursuits on hold for an unsure thing. That is stupid, and that is one of the reasons why some of us suffer as women.

We do not have our proper priorities set in stone. If we are that easily shaken from our agendas, then how will we ever know what we are made of? Women must realize that the first person for us should be us. If we do not stand firm in our own aspirations, agendas, dreams, and personal fulfillments, then who will? How can we expect love from a man who sees that we do not love ourselves?

Being able to love yourself is paramount, and it needs to be seen by your mate. What would happen if Janie delayed taking her dream job right away and then her boyfriend dumped her? How would she feel about herself then? Respect your dreams and hard work, and it will someday pay off. Women have to realize in this day and age that being independent is our only saving grace.

The time of having a husband to take care of us and to give us children when they see fit is fading away. Marriage still happens and still works, but how often is it successful? Why is that still what we are banking on? Happiness can only begin through the love of self. Making sure that you are self-sufficient and independent is an excellent start to finding yourself and your future happiness.

A great career and stable finances are extremely important to us all when we are seeking success and happiness, but being fulfilled is another requirement as well. Whether there is a great love or no one at all, we need to feel some sense of satisfaction from our everyday lives. Some women enjoy hobbies such as working out, sports, or traveling. Others may need to contribute something of value to others.

One of the reasons I wrote this book was to give back to others my experiences, mistakes, and victories in the hopes it would comfort and relieve anyone who is facing similar struggles. Knowing I have made a difference or a positive impact on someone else allows me to feel fulfilled and complete in ways I cannot explain. It is uplifting and validating to my soul to be of use or service to someone else.

Another perk in giving to others is that it takes your mind off your own problems and allows you to see that we all have hardships and pain. It helps you to realize that it usually does work out fine in the end. Whatever it is that gives you peace, resolve, and energy to make it through, use it as often as you can. We can never be too peaceful or too complete. It is an expanding circle that continually evolves.

Once you have established a stable existence for yourself, remember to focus on replenishing your spirit as well. We spend so much of our time trying to figure out and please others (our man, families, bosses, and friends) that many of us completely lose sight of what is pleasing to us.

Society is constantly telling women to think about, nurture, and love something or someone else more than we do ourselves. If it is not a man, it is children, and if it is not children, then it is an ailing parent or family member because we are single and childless. There is hardly ever a kind or tender word rendered to a hardworking, single, self-sufficient woman.

So regardless of your future circumstances, take the time out of your busy schedules to focus on the life you want for yourself. After you have established what you want, next figure out how to obtain this blissful existence. Eventually you will love, like, and accept the life you have chosen for yourself. It can happen if you just believe and take action.

Not all of us can be mothers and wives, and—news flash—many of us do not wish to be either. To all of the hardworking, single, childless women out there, I want you to know that I love you and you are totally all right to be who and what you wish to be. Love your life and let no one tell you that your life and ambitions should be anything other than what you'd have them be.

There are many women who choose to experience life completely differently. They do not want to have or raise children. The everyday rigors of raising a child may not be intriguing to all women. They may choose to help another person raise a child but not want all of the responsibility for themselves. Women have so many options now. We have become as resourceful as men now are. So find out what is intriguing to you and dive in feet first. Relish finding out who you are and what turns you on.

We all will hopefully one day realize that true happiness begins from within. Countless women have had children and were not happy with their mates or their kids. This is a direct result of these particular women not being fulfilled or happy with themselves. Many of us believe in order for us to be whole or considered a real woman, we must be a wife and mother first.

Well, for the record, how many women do you know of who were never angry or bitter about some aspect of their childbearing days? How many times have you heard another woman complain about how hard it is to raise children and have a life of her own? How many times have you heard a woman complain about how she gets no help from her husband or the children's father in raising them? One of our attributes, but also curses, is placing others' happiness before our own. Well, my dear friends, no matter where you reside inside of this spectrum of female experiences, know one thing: it is okay to be happy and in love with your chosen life.

A girlfriend of mine has had her life together since we finished college. She obtained her dream job straight out of school. She purchased her first home before the age of twenty-five, and she traveled at her discretion. However, she was constantly nagged by the women in her family to get a man and begin to settle down. Why? Why? Why?

We are programmed by the men and women around us to be selfless and unhappy. I am not suggesting we should not want to marry and have children but I am suggesting it is not the only solution to our problems. This is not the only goal or true pursuit of happiness for a woman anymore. Yes, most of us want to have children. and yes. we want a *good man* in our lives, but that is not the end of the story/ Be true to your life's dreams, goals, and aspirations first, and let everything else in life find you/

> *"Know what you want out of life and let no*
> *one and nothing sway you from it."*
> —Shannon Coursey

It takes a lifetime of experiences to fully comprehend yourself. Start listening to your inner voices and learn to trust your decisions. If and when you make mistakes, do not fall off from your current agenda—get up and keep moving toward your aspirations. Let no one define or lay out what your future should be. Put stock in your power and your potential. Learn to fall in love with plan ole splendid you. This is the first step toward being powerful.

RECAP OF CHAPTER 2

1. Real power is being honest with yourself and knowing that changes need to be made, being fearless enough to make the changes, and loving yourself in the midst of all of the changes.

2. Realize who the most important person in your life is and protect her at all times.

3. Learning to become your very best friend is crucial.

4. Start listening to your inner voices and begin to trust them.

5. Learning to love you is a necessity in life and should be practiced on a daily basis.

STRENGTH

*"Take the first step in faith. You don't have to see
the whole staircase, just take the first step."*

—Dr. Martin Luther King Jr. (1929-1968)

This part of the reading is a bit challenging and maybe even difficult to accomplish, but it is within your grasp. You have to reach down deep inside, take a deep breath, and believe you are entitled to free yourself from the pains of the past. Stop allowing your past life power over your possibly enriched and peaceful future. Whether it is a bad childhood, low self-esteem, sexual abuse, an unwanted pregnancy, or no one to tell you they loved you or you're special, ladies, please find the strength to let go of it and find a way to love yourself in spite of the cards life has dealt you. Know you are not alone and we *all* have had some rancid experience we have had to get over.

A wise old woman once told me, "You cannot grow into an old woman without at least one asshole to screw you over and stand in your way." Remember that, ladies. Please realize that finding your inner strength is the part of life that illustrates to you just how fearless, determined, and unstoppable you are. Learning how strong we are is where we also learn the true sound of our own voices.

Are you singing with your new found strength, or are you still trembling with fear on the inside? Take the next step to finding your inner voice and strength. The choice is yours. Be brave and choose to be strong, fearless, and ready to take on anything, with or without a man.

Chapter 3
Stop Looking for Daddy

This chapter is for all of us still looking for Mr. Right to make it right from what Daddy left behind. Okay you're a youngster and lonely for a big strong man to tell you that you are smart, beautiful, talented, and most of all *loved*. This is what we all want as little girls: to be told how special we are by the man in our life. Some of us are so blessed because we get just that and without having to ask for it. It is as accessible to us as it is for us to have air to breathe.

Funny, though, how even some of these blessed girls still turn out screwed up searching for him in every other man she beds or weds. Well, ladies, it is this simple: you must play the cards you are dealt. Whether you have or had a great father or if you do not even know his name or his whereabouts; time is ticking. How much more time are you willing to lose? Yes, we do learn to love from our relationship with our parents, but again, we must first learn to love ourselves so we can deal with the cards that are thrown to us.

What would happen if there was never a kind word spoken to us from a man? What would happen if we never ever felt a tender hand to hold onto or a sweet kiss on our face or strong arms to hold us? It would be sad and often lonely, but would we keel over and die from it? *NO!* The truth of the matter is there are many of us living right now who even prefer to be without the presence of a man.

This may sound frightening and maybe a little impossible for some, but we can and have survived without a man in our lives. It may not be what we are searching for, but it is the truth. It will be alright and it will still work out because, you know what, it always does. Knowing just this little fact will definitely aid some of you through the rest of this chapter.

In the following example, a young woman is searching for self-validation in the men she dates. She had a bad relationship with her father and desperately seeks attention from older men. Her fear is being left alone with only herself to depend on.

> *"Never allow fear to make your decisions for you."*
> —Dr. Tracy Smith

How many times have you heard of or seen a young woman dating a man twice her age? Usually this woman is rather attractive and viewed as being not very bright. However, she aligns herself with an older man who can provide her with something she thinks she cannot obtain on her own. It is usually money, notoriety, or possibly exposure to the finer things in life. He may also be a way out of a lifestyle that she hates or resents.

Her fear of being independent and self-efficient fuels this relationship. She has positioned herself to be taken care of and consequently controlled by her caregiver. She needs to realize that she can give herself the same thing, but she must first find her inner strength to go after it on her own.

Ladies, if this example rings true for you, please read on. Stop searching for a future including or pertaining to a man. We are programmed in many ways to seek a mate and to search for some kind of significance through a man. It all begins with our relationship or lack of a relationship with our fathers. We want a man to love us, make love to us, believe in us, support us, befriend us, trust us, and most of all complete us. We are looking to be told that we are beautiful, sexy, smart, brilliant, etc., etc., etc. *We need our egos stroked.*

Usually our fathers, the good and sometimes bad ones, come into our lives and validate us in some way. They tell us for the first time that we are pretty, smart, or special in some unique manner. We learn how to try to please a man and make him happy through interacting with our daddies. Unfortunately, if we are not mature enough, we tend to miss out on the messages that our fathers give to us.

In my case, I have a beautiful relationship with my daddy, but I was not smart enough in my younger years to pay heed to all of the signals that he demonstrated to me. My father showed me that a man is devoted to his family, putting nothing and no one else before them. He also showed me that a man will work as many jobs as needed to provide and protect his most prized possessions, his family and his home.

A good man is someone who is honest and knows how to show you what he is thinking and feeling. My father taught me all of these things, and he made sure to illustrate to me that a man should have some form of faith and belief in a higher principle (God). I love my daddy, and more than that, I respect him. Knowing all that he taught me still surprises me in how I chose my ex-husband. Somehow I went out and found the exact opposite of what my father stood for and believed to be true as a man.

What we are all wishing and longing for in our mates or future mates is to be loved wholly and completely by a man in a way we think our fathers should have or did. This, of course, is not realistic because our fathers loved us as fathers should, not as a man will. It is not feasible to believe that the protected, shielded, and selfless love of our fathers will be delivered to us from any other man.

Do not misunderstand me, ladies. Should a man love us in a selfless manner? Absolutely, but how often if ever does anyone love like that anymore? What I am proposing is that there should be a standard that we set for ourselves and for the man that we choose to love. This standard can be set at any time in our lives.

Young girls often fantasize about what their knight in shining armor will be like. Many of us who have close relationships with our fathers may give this knight some, if not all, of the attributes that our father possesses. *Setting the standards for your future mate is all fine and good, but you have to know one very important person first. This person, of course, is you.*

How do we know what we need and how we need it if we do not know who we are? This may sound strange or even ludicrous, but most of us, especially in our twenties and even later in life, do not know what we want or need. We also tend to ignore what irritates and annoys us. We often fail to notice what we cannot tolerate once we think that we are in love.

In the following example, a young woman tries to deal with her trust and low self-esteem issues. She purposely sabotages her relationships in fear that the man will betray her or leave. Being mistreated is a part of life. However, how a girl deals with this occurrence is what's most important.

Jessica is a thirty–year-old professor at a prestigious university in New York. She is considered by most of her peers and colleagues to be intelligent, attractive, and a great overall catch. Unfortunately, Jessica seems to have difficulty holding on to a man. She had a problematic relationship with her father and views men as cheaters and womanizers.

Whenever Jessica enters into a relationship, she immediately believes that her boyfriend will either cheat on her or leave her, so she typically does it to him before he can do it to her. Jessica knows that she has trust issues and low self-esteem from her initial relationship with her dad. Her belief is "I had better do it to him before he does it to me."

Intimacy and trust issues usually come from our primary relationships. How is it possible to be so successful but still have a dysfunctional habit such as this one? Women love to hold onto pain. Many of us have subconsciously learned to internalize our disappointments, hurts, and frustrations. Letting go of the pain and realizing that Daddy was human and also a jerk seems too easy for some, but it really is not.

Many of us listen and believe all of the negative things about ourselves in life instead of the more positive ones. It is as if the bond between pain, anguish, and disappointments is much sweeter to us than finding and holding onto real productive love. We embrace these negative beliefs and experiences until we ourselves become promoters of negativity and pain. It is strange to me how some of the most successful women still fall prey to listening and believing negative people from their pasts.

We all need a reality check in most of our relationships. Daddy is supposed to make things better and right for us, but what happens to a girl when Daddy was not around or was an extremely problematic guy himself? What is a girl to do when she has no man to look up to or to rely on? Where do we find our strong hands and shoulders to rest our heads upon when we have no *real man* to protect and shield us from the dreadful happenings of everyday living? We must rely on ourselves and remember that what others have done or may be doing has nothing to do with how we should love and perceive ourselves.

How we handle what life has offered us is very important and relevant to being a healthy and productive woman. Many of us have had extremely unfair and disastrous events happen in our lives. Sometimes we do need to seek help for what is troubling us. Sometimes time is the key to healing from our painful pasts. Whatever is necessary to be healed, know that we all have pains from our past and that if I can overcome them, so can you. Unfortunately, the young woman in this next example allowed her dreadful past and her father's addictions to determine her future.

> *"Bad things happen in life, but please never*
> *allow them to paralyze you."*
> —Angela White

A young girl lost her mother at the age of fifteen. Her father has a drinking problem and has never really been present in her life. She feels lost and, of course, realizes that she is alone. Her father steps up to the plate and tries to become a positive presence in her life. While having a weak moment, he slides into a drunken sleep at the home during a house party with some friends.

His daughter is violently raped by one of his close friends while he is in a drunken sleep. The friend tells her that her father will not believe her if she were to tell. The pain is so enormous she knows that she could not live with this abuse and look at her father anymore. She runs away from home and begins a life of drugs and prostitution. She has lost all hope of finding anyone she can trust or love. She is left with the belief that she must now use someone first before she is used again. Her self-worth and pride are killed along with the memory of the beautiful girl she once knew and loved.

This example happens to many of us, more than we would like to admit or speak of. However bad a young girl's situation is, there is power in the truth. The truth of the matter is that you were dealt an unfortunate fate at that time in your life. I am not diminishing at all what has happened, but why not turn a negative occurrence into a victorious ending? There are many successful and well-adjusted women who were victims of rape, physical abuse, and even molestation.

Instead of looking to replace a person who wronged you by another person or constantly seeking out the love that we missed in our childhoods, why not learn to love ourselves? This is no easy task or journey to take, but if we are ever going to be happy and content within ourselves, we must first love who we are.

Whether you are a victim or a success story, it all begins with you. This is a fact that cannot be preached enough. This young woman had to lose her mother and then be raped by a so-called friend of the family. She has no one to stand up for her or to protect her. Her back is up against the wall. Who is going to love her?

The only person qualified to love her is herself. The love of self for me is first truly found by the love of God. If God loves us just the way we are, then why can we not love ourselves? There are many of us who will never have a physical father here on earth, but that does not mean that we do not have a real man to look over us and to protect us when we cannot protect ourselves.

Whether there is a man or no man at all in your life, find a relationship first with God, and everything else will eventually work itself out. I am not saying that it will be easy, but at least there will be someone to talk to and to share your life with in those late-at-night times and all of the in-between times of any other relationship that you are vested in. Many times when we feel the most alone is when a relationship with God allows us to better understand ourselves and to clearly see a way out of our troubles.

There are so many of us that seek refuge in a bottle of spirits or some form of a drug, and we all should know by now that it is useless to do so. Why not try to find peace and solace in meditation and prayer with God? Learning to pray will allow us to let go of pain, confusion, disappointments, and anger. It has been proven that prayer changes negative situations into positive and successful outcomes.

These things that I speak of have helped me in several areas of my life. I married when I was twenty-four years old. Like most other young brides, I thought that I had figured out how love is supposed to work. I have an excellent relationship with my daddy, but for some strange reason, I did not properly choose the right man for me.

I spent many years wishing and praying that my husband would become more of a man like my daddy. I cried myself to sleep many a night wondering why he was not at home with me and why he could not love me like my daddy did. What exactly does that mean? Well, for me, it meant being loved in a protected sense. My father made me feel safe and secure, as if no one could harm or demean me. My daddy made me realize later on that it was unfair to expect any man to love me in the way that he does. I heard his words, but I still went on trying to turn my husband into such a man.

It was not until we had been married five years that it dawned on me that in order for anyone to love you in the manner you need to be loved, you must first love yourself. I knew that I did not like me, and I certainly did not love me. How could I find real love if there was no love for myself within? I began to soul-search and to seek a relationship with my creator, my originator, so that I could better understand my purpose, myself, and my future. Many times we are placed in bad situations or we pursue bad situations because we simply have to learn more about ourselves and life. Once we master that area in our life, we can then inspire or aid another lost person or soul.

No matter how hard we try to find daddy in a new love or lust that we meet, we have to first understand that there is an order to loving and being loved. First and foremost, we must love ourselves and understand what makes us tick before some man can come along and claim the prize. That's right, I said it—"the prize." Ladies, we are all just that, a prize. We are precious, significant, unique, and worthy of being loved, admired, and adored.

For the record, if the man you are seeing right now does not make you feel at least one of these things, then maybe you need to reconsider what you are seeking in this relationship. To all of the ladies who were not fortunate enough to experience being a "daddy's girl," let me say this: A good daddy makes you feel precious, adored, and revered all at once. If the man in your life does not provoke this feeling or make you smile at the thought of this experience, then again I say," Reconsider this relationship."

Now about what my father told me about the manner in which a man should love you: It is not feasible to seek in a romantic relationship what you had or missed out on with your father or lack of one, because a daddy should and usually does love you unconditionally. This is a rare type of love and is not meant for a romantic kind of love. We are *all* usually in a relationship for some kind of gratification or personal pleasure.

The average relationship over time will reveal all parties, including flaws and/or dysfunctions. So please do not think that the average man will see you as your father does or did. He will get to know you from a different type of intimacy. However, he should still see you and treat you as if you are precious and worthy of being loved just because you are a human being who is in an intimate relationship.

Why does intimacy matter so much in a real relationship? It is the channel in which we learn, discover, and find out if we can love one another. Intimacy allows us to truly show our mates who we are and how we became who we are. How many successful relationships are there without intimacy? I think most would agree that there are none.

This is what most females are searching for—intimacy. I am not referring to a sexual intimacy either. I am referring to a close and spiritual connection with a person. We all need to feel connected, heard, and more than anything, understood. Many times I hear my own girlfriends and other women talk about their men and how "he just does not listen." Listening is one of the ways that we become intimate.

The first man I was ever intimate with, like many of you, was my daddy. We cuddled, wrestled, kissed, and talked. I would talk with my father as a young girl, and he became my introduction to talking and sharing with a man. I looked up to my daddy in the physical and mental notion of looking up to your man.

I needed his opinion and his feedback on almost everything I did. I loved our talks and spending time together. He was my mentor, friend, and parent all wrapped into one person. My father possessed the attributes that I should have been seeking in my husband, boyfriend, or lover, but instead, I settled for what was is in front of me instead of what I knew within myself was true for me.

You and only you know when enough is enough and when it is time to move on with your life. Find the *strength* to say good-bye to the missed daddy from your childhood and move forward. We have chatted about a few things pertaining to our past and the pain that may be inhibiting us from really living. Ladies, I beg of you to try to let go of and stop the pains from your past. Life will never be sweet to you until you bury your painful past.

Learn to dance to your own music and stop relating happiness and wholeness to the man that is or is not in your life right now. Your Mr. Right could be closer than you think once you find the strength to let go of your long-gone past pains and embrace the possibly joyous future ahead of you. Remember: successful women are women of power and strength. It takes a hell of a woman to accept her painful past and yet shake it off and never allow it power over her again. Let tomorrow be the first day that your past does not affect your future.

RECAP OF CHAPTER 3

1. Find the strength to let go of the pains of the past.
2. Begin each day as an opportunity to be free from a burden or hardship you have experienced.
3. Stop looking to others for validation and love. Look for it from inside.
4. Learn to forgive others, but most importantly yourself.
5. Learn that a beautiful tomorrow begins inside of you today.

Chapter 4
Competition Is a No-No

Why do we feel the need to compete with one another for the love of a man? Many of us feel that there are not enough men out there or that it is too hard to find a man, let alone a good one. Well, interestingly enough, if we all made a conscious effort to *select* a man that is made for us and not for someone else, then we would all be in a better place. Why have women forgotten who picks whom? Why have we women turned our powers over to our male counterparts?

These are very serious matters that have to be addressed and answered in order for there to be true progress. How we perceive ourselves will ultimately determine how we end up in every relationship. If you think of yourself as worthy and deserving of a respectable relationship, then eventually that is what you will find. Consequently, if you think little or less of yourself, then that is what you will pull in. When we think the latter, we are subject to any and every kind of abuse.

Being in competition with another woman is only the tip of the iceberg in regard to our self-esteem and our self-perception. If we feel the need to compete with anyone other than ourselves, we are without a doubt in need of a self-esteem check. There is only one true race to finish, and that is the race of the human experience. Yes, we should try to experience as much as we can in this life in order to find and understand ourselves, but when we are faced with constant competition with others, we are secretly screaming within that we need approval, validation, and the attention of others.

These things are needed when we do not already know our worth or our mission in life. When we are playing on someone else's playground, we are usually thinking that theirs is better than ours. This is one of the reasons that we will date or sleep with another woman's husband or boyfriend. We fear going out there and finding a man of our own. So we make excuses to ourselves to take or borrow another woman's happiness.

Deep down inside, we all need to feel special, important, and for some of us, superior to others. If we cannot feel this on our own, then we will position ourselves in such a way as to get it from whomever. Some of us have absolutely no problem with getting this attention and adoration from a married man or a man committed to someone else. Most of the time, such women are completely unaware of their low self-esteem and are just trying to get their needs met as a woman.

I have a few girlfriends who have at one time or another dated married men or men in supposedly committed relationships. *Every one of these ladies who have dated married men has told me they had no knowledge of their own worth or needs.* They were just trying to get their egos stroked, or other things they may have needed at the time (such as money, travel, or nicer clothes).

If a woman is doing something without knowledge of her own worth or needs, then why is she doing it? What is she getting from the experience? We all find ourselves in life doing things we do not agree with or understand completely, but yet we still do them for some strange reason. Usually it is to earn some type of acceptance, love, or validation. The next example illustrates this situation.

> *"Most young women do not know their worth or potential."*
>
> —Carolyn Johnson

Tina is a twenty-two-year-old woman having an affair with a forty-year-old married man. She knows it will not last and that she is getting nothing from the exchange but an escort to certain events her job has her attend. Tina witnessed her mother's agony during several years of affairs her father participated in. As a young girl, she vowed she would never allow a man to treat her that way.

In her mind, she views fidelity and marriage as a farce. Tina's attitude is, "If I am going to get screwed over, then I might as well get something out of it." Whether she enjoys it or not, Tina is out for Tina and only Tina. However, slowly but surely, she is becoming more and more reluctant to continue the affair. Her mind and heart are no longer enjoying the pain of being the other woman. Tina begins to feel used every time they make love and he runs home to his wife.

Reality has a way of showing us the truth even when we choose not to acknowledge it. The manner in which we are reared and the values that make up our culture all contribute to how and why we live in the situations we find ourselves in. Tina witnessed her mother and father's relationship and the insane culture that it developed into. The daily exposure to her parents' relationship made an enormous impact on Tina and her views of love, trust, and intimacy.

As a young girl, I was told repeatedly that sex before marriage was wrong and a sin. I also remember my mother telling me that if a woman had nothing, she could always get a man. "The last thing in the world you should fear is getting a man; you can get one if you don't even have a dime in your pocket." My parents raised me to be a thinker and to depend on myself. They never portrayed or suggested in their parenting style the importance for me to need intimacy from a man. I was not taught to need a man for anything.

What I remember most about my parents' relationship were the intellectual debates, the long bouts of silence after the fighting ended, and the lack of affection they had for one another. I still to this day am not sure how I have internalized all that I learned from them as a married couple. What I am certain of is the standards they set for me as a woman. My parents shaped and governed my blueprint of relationships very subtly. Most of it was done, I believe, without their own knowledge of it.

I know their relationship left some kind of image with me about intimacy. There are invisible deeply rooted imprints of dysfunctional intimacy left somewhere within me. We all have pieces from our parents' battlegrounds embedded within us. Our parents contribute to our structuring of our own relationship cultures.

My culture when I was living at home with my parents was geared toward young women going to college and being self-sufficient. My rearing did not instruct me to find a man and expect him to take care of me. My parents also instructed me that if a man was committed to another woman, then he was off-limits. The point in all of this is that everyone has some idea of how a relationship works from first viewing their parents' relationship. Whomever you were raised with had an impact on your current beliefs about relationships.

My parents were not the only unhappily married couple to play out their lives in front of a viewing audience (me). They were doing the best they could at that time. It would do me a grave disservice to live out my life based on my parents' mistakes or unfortunate choices. Many of us have had poor examples or experiences of what love is. However, we cannot use that as an excuse forever. We need to become healthy in all relationships that we're a part of. We need to be complete in all areas of our lives. This can only occur once we know who we are.

The need to take what belongs to another woman is not representative of a powerful and strong woman. It is an example of a scared little girl. This girl is afraid to get out there and do the hard work of a powerful woman. She may be powerful at work. She may be powerful within other areas of her life. However, she is fearful of her full potential, and she is scared as hell of being alone. She would rather have only a piece of a man than to patiently wait for a real relationship to come along.

There are many reasons why women date married men. We need sex, affection, money, respect, conversation, and/or someone to spend time with. However, it is always the same ending: the woman is alone again and usually worse off than when she began. This type of relationship rarely ever prospers, and yet we are still allowing it to occur. Why would you do something that you know will only bring about more problems? It is easy for many of us to ignore the signs. We simply do not believe it will happen to us. We refuse to see that we, too, will lose at this game.

It is apparent that many of us hold nothing sacred anymore. Many of us are only out for ourselves. Too many times I have heard women say, "Hey, if she cannot keep up with her man, then that is her problem. If she messes up, I will pick it up." Whatever happened to us looking out for one another or simply leaving a family man and his family alone?

In the following example, Michelle is not happily married and wants more from her life. She knows her marriage will not last. So she decides to ruin her life as well as the others around her. If she is going to be unhappy, Michelle has to take a few down with her.

Michelle is a twenty-four-year-old woman who is on the verge of a divorce. She still loves her husband, but she knows he is weak and immature. All her life she has watched her mom deal with her father's wandering eyes and hands. Secretly Michelle believes her father was the happiest when he was with his other women.

The main reason she wants a divorce is because of her husband's indiscretions with a woman she knows socially. Michelle feels she needs to feel desired and sexy again. She has no children and knows her marriage will soon be over. At her office there is a young man named Derrick, whom she works very closely with. Derrick is newly married and seems somewhat happy. Their work keeps them together for hours on end.

They begin to converse casually at work and realize they are attracted to each other and share many things in common. They try to refrain from their mutual attraction and remain colleagues. Slowly but surely, Michelle works her way into Derrick's life. Derrick knows he is falling for her, but he thinks that he can keep it under control. Michelle has even gone to Derrick's home for dinner a few times with her husband and Derrick's wife. They all like each other and begin to hang out from time to time.

Eventually Michelle and her husband divorce, and she moves in for the kill with Derrick. She cries on his shoulder and even cries to his wife a time or two. In the back of her mind, she feels as if it is okay because someone else had done the very same thing to her. Michelle thinks it is now her turn to get over on someone. In her own little twisted mind, she thinks this will remove some of the hurt and pain she has suffered from her failed marriage.

Have we become so engrossed in our own lives that we no longer care about a family's lifestyle or what belongs to someone else? I have seen and heard of women who have affairs with their girlfriends' husbands, their sisters' husbands, and even their mothers' and aunts' husbands. This is a far cry from just simply being alone and lonely.

We have become angry, jealous, and yes, downright desperate. We no longer think or feel for another woman who may have found a good man and companion to enjoy her life with. The only thing that matters to us is us and what we need to believe and feel.

How many times have you been out with a lonely friend and heard her say things like, "I need a man to tell me he loves me, or I need to hear that it will be alright, or better yet, I need someone to lie to me tonight." We all are in need of tenderness and love, but for some strange reason, we will settle for lust and lies.

How can a powerful woman reduce herself to a mere roll in the hay with a married man? How does she sink so low as to accept a weekend every other month to feel sexy, appreciated, and yes, ladies, loved? Why do we constantly compromise ourselves for a simple kind word, a brief sexual encounter, or a few dollars?

Real *strength* comes from doing what is right even when every part of your body is dying to do wrong. Being strong is not easy, nor is it fair in many cases. Many times it involves little fun and no instant gratification. Being strong instills in us character, and it promotes integrity.

One of the reasons men treat us as sex objects is because we market ourselves as sexual objects. We do all the right things by attending top-notch universities and obtaining many of the goals we have made for ourselves, and yet we still reduce our worth to the man that is or is not in our lives. We will create our entire lifestyle for the hopes of finding love and acceptance from a man.

We become skilled in areas to catch a man. There are many of us who use business, our beauty, knowledge of what men want, and, of course, sex to ensure we land a man. Most women believe in order to hook a man these days, she has to be versed and highly skilled in sex. We still do not understand that sex is just a mere fraction of what we are and what we have to offer.

Many men do have relationships with women just for sex. I have heard men say that if it were not for sex, they would not have any need for a woman. These are men who use women for whatever it is they need at the present time. The ones who are only concerned with getting their own needs met.

Now, if you are the other woman and you are getting something out of it—for example, a college education, a paid-for home, or even a new car—at what price are you getting that supposed luxury? Are you trading in your soul, sanity, and body for this exchange?

I know of several women who were the other woman, and they have all told me of their regrets and the price they paid to only have a piece of a man, the mental abuse, and the emotional side effects of having an affair. They all told me of the heartbreak and constant fear of never truly having this man completely to themselves. They all spoke of being consumed and the unbearable notion of being alone forever.

Many times the men that they have these affairs with provoke the competitive natures of female relationships. All too often they try to compare their wives or girlfriends to the other woman. They will tell them such things as: "You are so much more giving and understanding than my wife." "After my wife had the kids, she just could not get her figure back. I love how you stay in such great shape." This one is my favorite: "Since we have had kids, my wife just doesn't like sex as much."

We have allowed men to control and manipulate us since the very beginning of time. We compete for our fathers' attention with our mothers and sisters. We compete with our friends for the popular guy in school or for the quintessential bad boy. How much longer are we going to be persuaded by others and choose not to listen to our inner voices? Being a sex object or using sex to feel love—or simply getting a quick fix to romance—is no longer the answer to being lonely.

Ladies, we need to stop being second-best and the buffer to whatever problems a man has at home or within himself. I am not sure how many of you have already learned this lesson, but if and when you do claim this man as yours, you will never feel safe or secure within his arms. Feelings of trust and security can only come from a person who you know is there for you and you alone. You will always be waiting for him to do to you what he did to his ex-wife or girlfriend.

There will never be an assuredness in his voice, touch, sentiment, and actions. How can you trust a man who has lied in front of you to his wife about where he was or what is keeping him out so late at night? How can you trust a man who only wants to see you when you are undressed and near a bed, a man that you never see in broad daylight for more than an hour or two at a time? When will you grow tired of not meeting all of his friends and family? When will you grow tired of spending holidays and many weekends alone or with your girlfriends?

This situation bothers me tremendously because we have spent years watching others—our parents, friends, and neighbors—live this lie. But yet and still, we are living it, too. Sex is not the only way to finding love. If it is, then what is going to happen when the sex changes—and believe me, it will.

Some of the sexiest and most beautiful women in the world live with and are married to men who cheat on them. Love and commitment are not established through good sex. Ladies, we have to realize that love is first a gift, and that gift will only be real to us once we first love ourselves. We all need to be loved, but at what price are we seeking it? Do we need to steal another woman's happiness to feel beautiful, desirable, and loved?

No matter how accomplished, beautiful, and successful you are, a man may still treat you badly or less than you deserve to be treated. We should all make a decision to end this insulting behavior and assume some kind of responsibility to put an end to it. If we know who we are and what we deserve, then no amount of anything (gifts, money, affection, attention, validation) should allow us to live below what we know to be our very best way of living.

To the ladies that do not agree with me and think that taking another woman's lifestyle and family away from her is exciting and an ego boost—to these ladies I say, "What goes around always comes around, and believe me, payback is a bitch." Another thing to remember: If he is such a good catch, then why is he cheating? Why are you constantly making excuses for where he is and how he disappears on you? Why are you so jealous of the time he spends with his wife and family if he really doesn't love her? Why are you sitting around waiting for him to call you? If he is such a great catch, why are you taking her sloppy seconds and thirds?

Think about it, girls.

"Real love does not make you feel needy or desperate."
—Angela Robinson

LABELS, LABELS, LABELS, LABELS

Why do we find the need to label ourselves and the women we know? Why do we refer to another woman as a good girl, a hoochie, a slut, a gold digger, a home wrecker, a bitch, or a whore? We do this because society has labeled us as such, and it is yet another way for us to feel superior and special over one another.

I am not talking about in fun when we are out with our girlfriends and the word bitch is often used as a term of endearment. I am talking about when we do it out of anger and malice for another woman. I do not care if you are a virginal schoolteacher or a call girl for hire, you are first and foremost a woman. No matter where you are in life, you need to be able to look at yourself in the mirror and be okay with where and what you are. If you cannot, then you have some work ahead of you to do. Please, ladies, stop searching for validation in any person other than you.

Most of us at some point in our lives will play the role of schoolgirl, mother, freak, bitch, and snob. Please do not think that you are above any other woman walking the street trying to make it and looking to be loved. The bottom line is we are all the same; none of us should ever try to feel superior or above any other woman living the human experience.

Stop the pettiness, ladies, and let's get to the important stuff. We need to heal ourselves first and next learn to help others heal. Stop fighting one another, and instead, reach out and help each other grow and become prosperous. It is time for us to make it right with each other so we can then go and make it right with them (men).

We cannot fix our problem with men until we fix our problems within ourselves. I hope we can all stop and make this our first priority. We will all be better off if we simply put our need to be loved in our own hands.

Another thing we do is compare our beauty or lack thereof to other women. We do this all of the time. Asking stupid questions like, "Do you think she's prettier than me? She has such great legs, I hate her." Why do we refuse to see our own inner beauty and stop the competing? The reason we do this is that we are human and it is normal to feel insecure and self-conscious at times—but it shouldn't be to the point that we forget or lose ourselves in someone else.

Most magazines hope and pray that we will always be more interested in another person's life than in our very own. They tell us to be thinner, richer, happier, sexier, and, yes, in love forever. This is the real world, and we must be real with ourselves every single day in order to accept, embrace, and love our very own existence.

Think about some of the most beautiful and successful women in the world, and most of them will tell you that they focus from the inside out. They are usually more focused and centered on their inner strength and beauty. Success will only come to you from first knowing yourself and then from believing in your own personal gifts and powers that God has blessed you with.

However long finding out who you are takes, it is the single most important next step to make. Some of us are lucky enough to find the love of our life sooner rather than later. However, most of the more successful unions between man and woman begin with each player being whole and complete before the union takes place. So, ladies, getting to know who you are is the first and most important step to finding Mr. Right. I have all the faith that you will first find you and then allow him the opportunity to find you.

RECAP OF CHAPTER 4

1. You should only compete with you; no other woman's possessions or achievements should ever be coveted.

2. We need to support and encourage all women through challenging times; negativity is counterproductive to future gains as women.

3. Learn who you are and what you are made of before you search for Mr. Right.

4. A woman of real *strength* focuses on life from the inside out, not the outside in.

5. Focus on loving you first, and Mr. Right will eventually show up.

Chapter 5
What Matters the Most

Over and over again, we think that having a man and being in love is what counts the most. Over and over again, we learn how erroneous this notion is. Why do we often hear the clichés that there are other fish in the sea or time heals all pains? The reason for these sayings is that people all too often experience heartbreak and loss at love. We as women place so much value and weight on our relationship status. If we are in a relationship, we nitpick it apart in regard to the seriousness of the union or the possibilities of a promising marriage.

If we do not have a man or the hopes of one, then we obsess over where he is and how soon we can find him. No matter how prosperous we are or how fulfilled we are in other areas of our lives, if there is no relationship, then we feel there is no wholeness or happiness. Ladies, why do we place our happiness and wholeness in the hopes of a future mate or companion? That is the topic of this chapter: Why do women value companionship more than happiness and peace?

Peace is the key to all things; without it, we can do nothing successfully. Now I know that many of you are not seeing the whole picture, but this is very true for us all. Peace occurs when we are comfortable with who we are and totally at ease when things are not going the way we would like them to. My mother used to tell me all the time that without peace, there is no clarity. This would always cause me to think about my relationships because that was where most of my problems were.

I was a good student, and my friends back then were the same friends I have right now. So why would I immediately obsess over or about my relationship with a man? The answer is simple now, but it was very perplexing back then; I knew deep down inside that my romantic involvement was a tad bit askew and different from what I was searching for. Why did I settle and stay in a dysfunctional relationship? I stayed because of fear, loneliness, and trying to appear like I had it all.

We all at some point or another get caught up in appearances. We women try so hard to have the perfect home, career, and, of course, man. We all want that ideal man. I was no different. Deep down inside, I thought that if I had a great guy, it meant I was together as a woman. Similarly, many of us also tend to think if our mate is no good or he is bad for us, then we are the same or viewed as the same.

The shame of choosing the wrong mate for ourselves burdens many women into staying with a man she knows is no good for her; she will remain just to save face. It is ludicrous and absurd to think that if we choose poorly, we must stay, suffer, and remain quiet about it. We think we can keep this problematic relationship hidden in order to keep alive the image we believe we have created for ourselves. I failed to realize like many other women that self-preservation and being able to live the fullest life possible was slowly leaving my grasp. It was slipping away because of an image I wanted to portray.

Why do many of us sacrifice our own happiness for others'—our children's, our mate's, and other family members? This is a female characteristic I cannot understand. If we are to change our options and future outcomes, then we must first and foremost save ourselves from ourselves. We need to stop suppressing our true feelings and become as honest as possible with ourselves. Then and only then can we understand what our real problem is and figure out how to resolve it.

Whatever your real problem is, know that you are not alone or the first to encounter this dilemma. Know also that in time it can be resolved. Time has a funny way of maturing us and showing us that we will be okay and we will get over it. The old saying that what doesn't kill you will only make you stronger is so very true. I have found it to be bittersweetly true.

No matter how bad things became in my marriage or while I was dating my ex-husband, I always came out stronger, more confident, and much more prepared for the next boxing match, whether it was minuscule or huge in relation to other battles. It all starts from the onset from within. If you know that you are suffering from depression or low self-esteem, or if you are scared to death of being alone, know one thing, my sister: there is only one you, and only you can set things straight in your life—no one else can or will.

Now there may be a person to inspire you or uplift you, but it still resides in you to make a change or a difference in your life. If there is one notion or thought that I want each and every woman to feel and to know about herself, it is to *first fall in love with yourself.* This is a hard concept to finesse when you do not have a narcissistic disorder, but it can be accomplished. We should all love ourselves the same way in which we love or cherish those special someones in our lives.

Most of us have at least one person whom we love unconditionally, completely, and selflessly. For me, it is my children. I want the very best for them, and I hope that they have everything that is good and rightly deserved by them. I would never want them to be hurt or disappointed by some undeserving man in their lives. The moment a man could not provide them with the love, nurturing, and support they rightly deserve, he would have to go in my opinion. Now that is exactly what I should also want for myself. Why would I believe I deserve anything less than that?

Vanessa is a great looking girl who knows what she wants in life. She has a great career and a very supportive family, but for some strange reason, Vanessa thinks that in order to be loved or liked by a man, she has to compromise herself and sleep with him well before she even knows him. Her mother told her very little about men since she raised Vanessa as a single mother and worked most of the time just to make ends meet.

Most of the women around Vanessa were either divorced or they had never married and lived alone. Vanessa learned about relationships mostly from her high school male friends. She was told that in order to keep a guy interested, she had to give it up and give it up quickly. So now Vanessa is thirty years old and is wondering what is wrong with her because she has yet to marry or remain in a relationship for more than a year and a half. She has slept with most of the men at her job and is not happy or proud of her current social status.

Why do we try and try to change a man and not ourselves? We insist upon making him into what we want, but we resist evolving into a more self-sufficient woman. How is it that each and every day we overlook or deny the flaws that we possess? Ladies, there are many dysfunctions we are tolerating and accepting that we possess ourselves.

For the ladies who are suffering from low self-esteem, what would be better than believing in yourself and knowing what your worth is? Many of us do not even know that we have low self-esteem. Well, here are just a few clues as to whether or not you are dealing with this issue. Do you feel awkward around most people and wonder if they can see your flaws? Do you usually place more importance on other people's needs, desires, and thoughts than your own? Do you constantly worry about your looks or over exaggerate your flaws? Do you daydream of looking, acting, or being someone else that you think has her life together?

Do you find yourself thinking of ways to be valued or loved by someone else? Do you feel that you are not whole if you are not loved by someone else? Do you typically use or think about using your body or sex to get the love or attention you need from someone else? Do you find yourself diminishing the achievements that you have made and glorifying the areas that need improvement in your life?

We all have these thoughts from time to time, but if your life is consumed by these thoughts, it is probable that you are suffering from low self-esteem. We as women place so much weight on what makes our man tick and so very little weight on knowing and loving every aspect of ourselves. How do you expect a person to love and respect you when you don't love and respect yourself? How can we be complete in a relationship with a man when we are not whole and complete alone?

Now, ladies, there are going to be some times when we have to be alone with ourselves. This is not a bad thing; this is great. It used to scare me to death to be utterly alone and separate from another human being. I had to have someone around me at all times. If it was not the comfort of my girlfriends, then it had to be the attention of my man. Conversation was a must for me.

One of the best aspects of my marriage (that I did not realize until later) was that my ex-husband left me alone quite a bit. It was difficult being a newlywed and being alone all of the time, but it eventually taught me how to be okay with being inside of myself. I had to listen to my private thoughts and filter out the good, the bad, and the ugly. It forced me to see myself and my ex-husband for who we truly were. It made me realize that there was nothing wrong with me other than having a little, no, a lot of low self-esteem.

Once I could admit it and deal with the fact that I played a major role in my abusive marriage, I could then do something about it. No one can be abusive or mistreat you unless you allow it. I allowed my ex-husband and many other people close to me in my life to disrespect and treat me badly. This was a long and hard revelation for me to conceptualize, but it was also one of the most liberating and uplifting awakenings as well.

If you are being mistreated or abused and want to change this situation, you must first believe that you do not deserve this circumstance. Then you have to understand that whatever you got yourself into took time. Meaning it will take time to resolve or dissolve your present situation. Make sure you are thinking clearly and soundly. Revenge sounds good, and the thought may even feel really good, but focus solely on you changing you. Do not factor in anyone or anything else at the time, unless of course you have children.

When I first began to see my faulty thinking and to reassess myself, I had several reasons to stop myself. I was fearful of the change, and I was a tad bit comfortable with my present situation. I knew that although I had a terrible marriage, my children were comfortable living at home with their daddy.

Many of you will have very similar and probably more serious excuses to remain in the pain, anguish, and idiotic state you are in. These fearful excuses and inhibitors are only prolonging what will more than likely occur. Each day I justified staying or trying one more time to make it work, I was only bandaging my wounds and allowing him to think everything was okay. The verbal abuse was okay. The infidelity was okay. The lack of respect was okay. The physical and mental abuse was okay. *Do not prolong your abusive future another day.*

We usually fear what is unknown to us. Many of us will stay in an unhealthy situation because it is familiar to us. We do not have to guess what will happen next because we know what the end result will be. Whatever that end result is, ladies, aren't you tired of it? Aren't you tired of holding it down for an undeserving man, a man who has never and probably will never see, respect, or love the woman you are? Stop making up excuses and get busy in preparing a new future for you and your family.

Finding your strength means you have to accept there were

some things that were not in place in your life. Whether it was a bad childhood, a bad marriage, or a bad sense of self, know that we must first love ourselves in the midst of all of these troubles and we must never compete, steal, or begrudge another woman's victories or accomplishments. The *strength of a woman* is found when she is at peace with herself and her past, prepared for the future, and conditioned to take whatever life has in store for her. Once we have the power to be who we are and the strength to be comfortable within our own skin, then we can find a peaceful place where we learn to forgive.

Recap of Chapter 5

1. Stop connecting happiness with companionship.

2. Fall in love with yourself first.

3. Finding inner *strength* is the onset to finding peace within.

4. Believe that you can redirect your current circumstances.

5. The *strength* of a woman has to be discovered so the Unknown Woman Within can be found.

Forgiveness

"Remember, the Lord forgave you, so you must forgive others."

—Colossians 3:13

There is truth in the saying that "we tend to forgive others easier than ourselves." Well, this portion of the reading is set up for forgiveness of others but mostly of ourselves. How can we grow and become better women if we still are holding on to anger, disappointment, and self-hate within ourselves? Well, the answer is that we can't. If God can forgive us our selfishness and ignorance, then why can't we? It takes time to learn from your mistakes, and it takes time to evolve into a better version of yourself. *Give yourself a chance to blossom.*

There is peace in forgiveness. So, learn from your mistakes and move on. Holding onto self-hate or hating someone else enslaves you to being a prisoner of the pain and suffering. Free yourself from it all and know that in life we all do stupid things but the successful woman falls and gets back up swinging. So, get yourself suited up for success and ready to move towards your soulful journey of finding your Unknown Woman Within.

Chapter 6
The Core of a Man

Maya Angelou once said, "When a person shows you who they are, believe them."

There are many of us who are already in a failing relationship, and we know we should end it. However, the fear of being alone or the security of having just a piece of a man hinders most of us from doing what needs to be done. When figuring out what is best for us, we often choose what *feels* good to us rather than what *is* good for us. Like our male counterparts, we all too often think with other parts of our anatomy. In the following example, Anita knows her mate of ten years is not the one; however, she remains in an unfulfilling relationship hoping that either her feelings or her mate's will change.

Anita was a thirty-year-old woman having her second baby with a man she had been dating for ten years. Their first child, a little girl, was only nine months old when they found out about the new baby. Upon having a conversation with one of her closest girlfriends, Anita told her she was not sure if she wanted to marry her boyfriend Damien of ten years because she was not sure about his core. This startled her friend because she

65

could not understand why Anita would continue in a relationship and bear his children if she still did not know him for the man that he was.

This scenario is one that frightens and saddens me to no end. Why do we make a man who we know is no good for us, the man of our lives—and even worse, the father of our children? This is a mental prison we create called self-abuse. Should I be alone or be enmeshed in a disastrous, possibly even deadly, relationship? The answer is emphatically not just no, but hell no. This whole thought process reeks of insanity.

First and foremost, Anita already knows and has known for quite some time that Damien is no good. She has seen it, and she has felt it for some time. Long before the first pregnancy, she knew he was not ever there for her when she needed him, but she decided to wait until the clouds from heaven opened up and God himself told her to get the hell out. Well, Anita honey, it ain't gonna happen.

He will be around as long as you will have him around. It is amazing to me how the bad ones stick like glue to ya. A good man will get the hell out faster than a speeding bullet. You know why he leaves quickly? He leaves because he is healthy, and you clearly are not. The bad apples unfortunately fester and stay because the two of you are feeding off of one another. Your insecurities and his idiosyncrasies bounce off of each other and make up a once-in-a-year happy home.

Every once in a while, you will see what you once saw in him that made you fall for him, and things will go swell for a few weeks, maybe even a month or two; but sooner or later, the real person has to resurface and rear up his ugly little head. You find yourself thinking *oh we are doing so good right now, maybe he has changed, calmed down, mellowed out, grown up, or even become saved.* Well, sometimes these things do actually occur, but for the most part, he is still whom he is and you are still who you are.

Our focus is often directed toward him instead of ourselves. Do we ever stop and think about what could happen if we changed our perspectives and consequently changed our options? My father has always said that we may never get exactly what we want in life, but we should try to have as many options as possible. Our options allow us better choices to select from and more freedom to pursue these choices. One of the reasons we fail to create more options is that we are afraid to change the recipe we think will bring forth a beautiful relationship in life.

How to keep him in my life recipe 101:

Put his needs before my own.

Take care of him, that is, give him money, sex, and my undivided attention.

Call him all the time, telling him that he is on my mind and in my heart.

Know what his hobbies are and incorporate them into my world.

Get to know his family and make sure they like me.

Blah, blah, blah, blah, blah.

If this was sickening to read, think of how sickening it was to know that I used to do those things without even knowing I had that type of an agenda. We all at some time or another have had a need to place him and his world ahead of ours. This mode of self-destruction is termed codependency. When we are afraid to empower ourselves and be whole as women, we tend to place our identities into the hands of our men, children, etc. I am not suggesting we should not show our love to a *good man* by cooking and doing nice things for him, but I am stating the facts: we must first see about our own needs before we can see about others' needs. Desperation, loneliness, and fear should not hold us to a man that we know has no idea or desire to reciprocate love to us.

How do we see through the nonsense and know the core of a man? How do we know what a good man looks, sounds, and feels like? Well, this is an old but yet simple question. First and foremost, you will never know for sure what he looks, sounds, and feels like to you until you know who and what you are and need. Most of us do want an honest, intelligent, attractive, hardworking, God-fearing, child-loving, faithful man of substance. These are all very vague and generalized characteristics. Let's make these notions more specific and more realistic.

The *businesswoman* (meaning a woman making a very good living) usually has a great five, ten, and twenty year plan for career and, of course, her finances. How well does she know herself? She has spent the majority of her adulthood being independent, aggressive, disciplined, and in total control of herself.

She has been chasing goal after goal after goal and has realized that she does not want to spend the rest of her life alone. She thinks a man may now be a proper addition to her life. She has no children and has thought in the past that she may not really want to have them. What type of man does she need? What would his core be like in order for her to let her guard down and try to develop a future with him? What qualities would he possess?

Well, I took the initiative to ask a friend of mine who fits this description of a successful woman, and here are her responses. The first thing that came to her mind in regard to a man's core was that he has to love life and know how to laugh. He must know how to relax and enjoy the life he is living. She did not feel he needed to have lots of money, be great looking, or be eager to take care of her. *"I would like to find a man who is self-sufficient and knows what he wants in life."* Notice that she did not say, "I am looking for a man" or "I need a man." Instead, she stated that she would like to find a man who has such and such. There was no urgency in her voice or in her expression, nor was there a fear of not having this for herself.

She already has what she needs to be fulfilled and complete in her life; therefore, she can now be open and allow the kind or type of man she wants and deserves into her life. There is a price we all must pay in order to be loved or involved in a relationship, but the price must be something you are happy and willing to pay. I hope and pray that my daughters are falling all over themselves trying to pay the right price because hopefully they will have chosen wisely and at the right times in their lives. Knowing a man's core is pivotal in choosing a mate, but knowing your own core and where your future is going is twice as vital.

The *stay-at-home mother* may have a different agenda. She knows her mate must be financially well-off because she wishes to be at home raising children. Even though this is a prerequisite, she still should have the resources to take care of herself if need be. Her ideal mate may not present himself until she is well into her thirties. If he never shows up in this day and age, she could possibly be on her own forever. These situations are real and happen every day, but how we prepare for them is crucial.

This lady may need a man who is hard working. Since she will be at home rearing children, she may need a go-getter, a man who will be loyal to his first priority, his family. This couple will need to see eye to eye on who will make the money and who will run the home. They should be a team in every stage and phase of their lives, from parenting to retirement.

They will have to be grounded and unified on topics from religion to when, where, and how much money they will invest and save. A stay-at-home mother must have a clear and sound understanding of her role as a wife and mother and also her future mate. She has a lot of homework to do when it comes to finding the man that will complete her agenda.

The *so-called gold digger* has a love for living life in the utmost luxury, and she knows what it takes to obtain this—a man with a lot of *money*. However, should she overlook everything else about him in order to secure her lifelong dream?

We are all searching at some time or another for a man that will add something special to our lives; but for some of us, we are searching for him to validate who we are. Ladies, wanting a man to walk this journey of life with is understandable. Looking for a mate to build a family with and live happily ever after with is also understandable. Needing a man to make all of the major purchases in your life is a *no-no*.

The thought of freeloading and expecting no heartaches and consequences is foolish. Stop wasting your time, girls. This may work for you before the age of thirty, but what happens after that? What happens when you have given all of your youth searching for a wealthy man and still have no proposal or the invites become few and far between? How much longer will it now take you to create an authentic life of your own?

No matter what your vision for the future is, knowing what type of man you are with is essential. The three women previously described all had an agenda in regard to their futures, and their agendas all included a man. The core of a man will tell you what to expect from him in uncertain times; it will hopefully assure you of his current and future agendas as well. Regardless of what he represents, if it is not complementary to your life, then reconsider making a life with this man. As Maya Angelou said, "When a person shows you who they are, believe them." Many times we discover early on in the game that a man is rotten to his core or simply just the wrong player to put in the game, but we insist upon keeping him in the game and hoping he will catch on and learn to play it our way. We spend too much time scheming on how to manipulate this man into being what we would like for him to be.

A dear girlfriend of mine has often told me of how men will come and pretend to be your ideal man; however, most of them have no desire to be anything more than Mr. Right Now. There is basically no way to truly know every part of a person without spending a lifetime with them, but we do have instincts to tell us (if we are smart enough to listen) when and how soon to get out.

These instincts have been with us from the very beginning of our existence, but for some odd reason, we allow love, fear, codependency, and hope to keep us in a union that we know is no good for us. One simple yet hard resolution to make is to accept a man for who and what he is and move on. A man's core is not always easy to see or to understand initially. We need to slow down long enough to know what it is we are searching for, and then we could be better positioned to intelligently select the ideal mate for us.

I have chatted with many women of all ages. The majority of them who are less than thirty years old believe life would be incomplete and unfulfilling if there were no husband or significant other within reach. Older women believe it would be nice to have male companionship, but they also state they feel a man can weigh a woman down or interfere with her finding and loving herself. My mother used to say to me all the time, "If you don't have a dime in your pocket, you can still get a man. The trick is, do you want him?"

Well, we could all benefit from an older woman's insight and mistakes. Finding out about your partner's core is all about finding out what you already know from within. If you need to find out a man's core and you have been dating him for over a year and a half, then the work has already been done; you just do not want to face the music. Funny how we can go out and purchase a new pair of shoes or a new outfit and if it looks good on us and is comfortable, we keep wearing those shoes or that outfit until they are worn, torn, or simply outdated. We know within the first wearing what's up.

Why are we so blinded when we're in a relationship? When our whole physical, mental, and emotional beings are telling us he is not good for or to us, why do we ignore it? What major signs do we need to get out of a problematic relationship?

We get married to Mr. Asshole and have Mr. Asshole's children, continually thinking it is going to work out or that he will change. We need to get a firm grip on our reality and realize what everyone else around us knows. The reason our family and friends no longer come around is because he is an asshole. Ladies, if the following example depicts your situation in any way, you can change it.

Nikki was twenty-two years old when she met Michael. They dated for two years and got married. Nikki knew from the onset that Michael was not the one for her, but she was ready to leave home and have a man take care of her until she could figure some things out for herself. Nikki had never lived outside of her mother's home, and she had only worked two jobs her whole life. She was not college educated and thought that college was not ever an option.

After they married, she soon became pregnant and felt safe in the fact that she would be a housewife. Michael told her to stay home with the baby and keep his tidy home in check. Nikki thought this was too good to be true. She became very comfortable in the life Michael was providing and thought this would never change.

Nikki had no idea Michael would begin to have affair after affair, nor did she realize eventually he would stop coming home and paying the bills. Her biggest fear is unfolding right before her unprepared eyes. Nikki will have to face the fact that Michael is not the man she had hoped for and take her comfortable ass to work.

All too often we become comfortable in our day-to-day living, and we begin to accept a life we did not set out to live. There are very few people who enjoy and are looking to be mistreated or abused. However, life has a funny way of placing us in certain positions where we are forced to choose the quality of life we desire. If we know what we want and have a firm idea of how to achieve it, then usually we choose well and wisely. Unfortunately, many of us have no idea what we want and we certainly have no clue how to get it, so we refrain from listening to the inner voice from within that is screaming *Get out and start over* or *Get the hell out fast and never look back.* That is how it happens.

> *"Love never disrespects you."*
>
> —LeVette Fleming

Nikki realizes Michael will never change and probably will never give her the life she needs, so she becomes frantic. Nikki has had many thoughts to leave and make it on her own with two kids and no education. Nikki always assumes it will take too much time, money, and discipline to make this notion work.

Every time she has a solution to one of her problems to get out, she finds another ten reasons why it still won't work out for her. She is sabotaging her internal fight within to survive and find happiness. She does not want to go back home and live with her mother, who has offered to help her get back on her feet. Now Michael is unemployed and hardly ever at home, and she is forced to either go home and make a way for her children or stay and find some other way to support Michael and their kids.

All of the warning signs were there. Nikki, however, chose to ignore them and hope things would work themselves out. She paid no attention to Michael's personality changes—coming home late night after night, spending money that could not be accounted for, picking fights to get out of the house, not having sex with her, and never wanting to talk or listen to her at all. Nikki remained in la-la land the entire time until the eviction notice came. She was scared to death. What would happen to her and her children? What would people think? What would Michael do if she left him? She never really thought about how happy and successful she just might be if she made a life on her own terms.

We have all done this to some degree in our lives. We focus on whatever we possibly can to avoid looking a mistake smack-dab in the face. We hold on so dearly to what our man used to be or could be, instead of what he is. We refuse to seek the love we need from within. Instead, we beg and plead for it from someone else, who we know cannot produce it and even if they tried, it still would not be enough. Ladies, the core of a man is important, but if there is no self-love, no self-respect, or no knowledge of self-worth, it is all in vain. He could be the greatest man walking, but until you know who and what you are made of, eventually life will throw enough curve balls that somehow, somewhere it will all go under.

No one, and I mean no one, can make you okay inside your own skin except you. I do not care how fine, tall, smart, hardworking, good in bed, or fun-loving a man is, if you do not know your core, then you are losing at the first hello. Invest in yourself, and your tomorrows will be okay. Invest in yourself, and your life will have peace and understanding. Invest in yourself, and your future will be brighter than any shooting star imaginable.

RECAP OF CHAPTER 6

1. Desperation and fear should never keep you in any relationship.

2. Stop living in the past and face your current situation smack-dab in the face.

3. Do what has to be done and move on forward with your life.

4. Pat yourself on the back for your newfound strength.

5. Invest in yourself by letting go of your past mistakes and believe things will get better.

Chapter 7
Let Bygones Be Bygones

Most of us at some awful point in our lives have been heartbroken and run over by what we think is love. We try to hang in there and fight for what we believe belongs to us, but many times we are left or forced to leave because the relationship has long been dead. How do we put it all back in place for ourselves and stay inspired to find true love? How do we refrain from being jaded for any future relationship?

Many of us jump right back into love or lust in a rebound attempt at a successful relationship. However, what we had and lost seems to haunt the new relationship. We find ourselves yearning for some of the past experiences we shared with our exes and comparing how different this new guy is from them. This is the cold hard truth: in order to be free of your past, you have to submit to the pain, accept the ending of it all, find peace with your current status, and move on with joy for having experienced the ride. Now this may seem too simplistic or even a bit elementary, but it does work.

Rachel had been in a degenerating relationship with Brian for three years. They had at one time spoken about marrying and having a real future together. Rachel had never had any real problems with Brian. He was good-looking, a professional man, STD free, and very attentive to Rachel's needs. His dream was to someday own his own bank.

Brian was very dedicated to his dreams and tried very hard to include Rachel in his dreams. Rachel was a nurse and had a very simple life. She was working at both a hospital and a nursing home and had made a very nice life for herself. They met through a mutual friend who thought they would be perfect for each other.

The problem in their relationship was they did not share the same dreams. Rachel wanted a 9 to 5 man who would be home to handle some of the duties of husband and father, and Brian wanted a woman who would jet set with him and allow his career and life to be her focus as well.

It was not until two years into the relationship after all of the newness had gone that they realized they loved each other but not enough to compromise on their dreams. Brian eventually told Rachel she could not live the life he was seeking and that he had meet someone he felt could.

This type of letdown happens quite often to many women. You find a man who has almost everything you want, but it just does not work out. What do you do to get back on your feet? How do you recover from a two-year relationship that everyone was sure would lead to marriage and happily-ever-after? The first thing to keep in mind is it took time to develop this union and it will take even longer to release it. Releasing a lifestyle or a person you loved is not an easy task to accomplish, but no matter what, it has to be done. If you refuse to let go, you will only deter yourself from the healing process and from possibly later being whole enough again to find love.

When I realized I was going to divorce my husband of ten years, it saddened me that my marriage was not going to be a happily-ever-after story, but I found a sense of relief in knowing I would no longer be in a union that made me feel unworthy, unattractive, and insecure. I was reluctant to rip my family apart and in denial of how ugly and difficult it would be to make this journey to freedom.

There are many emotions involved when you are starting over and radically changing your identity, but the two things I held onto were the facts that other women have survived divorce and that God would be with me every step of the way. I knew no one tried harder than me to make a marriage work, but sometimes you have to let bygones be just that—bygones—and move on.

All of the passion and rage that we had encountered in our marriage had left us, and we were two totally unhappy, numb, and unproductive people. Instead of me blaming him or even worse hating him; I decided to leave before I could no longer be humane to him in any way at all. I was letting go of my children's father, who I once thought was my friend and the best man in the world for me. It was not easy, but it had to be done in order for me to be whole and healthy. My children deserve a happy, sane, and fulfilled mother. I did not want them to see me as an insecure, abused, and indifferent-to-life woman.

When we are making final and heartbreaking decisions, we must hold onto the belief that the person we are longing to become or to see again will not appear if we remain in an unhealthy relationship. If you are trying to get out of a bad situation, start first by seeing yourself free, happy, and at peace in your life. Allow yourself to dream and to dream elaborately and frequently. Make it a part of your everyday rituals. Go to bed at night and wake up in the morning knowing you will not feel this troubled all the time and not for much longer. Know that each day will get a little easier, but also keep in mind there will be good days and yes, ladies, some really bad ones.

I had some days where I woke up crying and went to sleep crying, but I knew within my very being that it was the right decision and the only one that would grant me the peace and confidence I needed to be all that I could be. This is a part of living that we can only endure alone, but utilize every opportunity available to stay busy, focused, and centered on you.

Spend your time believing you will get past it and that one day you will be able to aid another poor soul who is struggling through the exact same thing that you are at this very moment. Life lessons are best served when we grow from them and in return help someone else with the process of evolving into a wiser and more compassionate person. What is the point of going through anything and not finding out something beautiful and beneficial to others? Many of you may read this and think, "There is no way I am ever going to forgive him, let alone grow from it." Well, if you do not learn from something that has almost destroyed you, it is quite possible you will experience it again and again until you do.

Lori was in college the first time she fell in love, and she fell hard, very hard. Lori was a very smart young woman and had some idea of what she wanted for herself and her future. Sometime during the first semester of her sophomore year, Lori fell in love with her psychology professor, Dr. Armstrong. Dr. Armstrong was known for finding a new pretty face and cultivating a whirlwind affair every other year he taught freshman psychology.

Many friends tried to discourage her from having this affair, but Lori had never felt this way before. This was the first time in her life that a man of importance and prestige paid her any attention and was offering her an intimate intellectual relationship. Most of the boys she had dated before were just that, boys, and could only hold her attention for a short period of time.

They spent all of their free time together and even dreamed about a future together. He introduced her to everything from Freudian theory to getting high and making love off of it. Lori did not care what anyone told her: she was happy and she believed they were all jealous and threatened by the twenty-two-year age difference they shared. Even when Samantha, his last conquest, told her all about his motives and agenda with her, Lori thought it would not happen to her. She was sure this was real and that Richard really loved her.

It was not until the following year that she could see him slowly slipping away. His calls became short and strained. He did not want her to spend so many nights at his place anymore, nor did he ever ask her out anymore. She did not know how to explain it, but deep inside she felt herself longing for him to tell her he loved her or just to be touched by him. It was as if she was going through some type of withdrawal.

Her actions became desperate and very similar to a drug addict's in the pursuit of getting one more hit. How did she lose control of this man who used to be wrapped around her fingertips? Finally Dr. Armstrong told her to leave him alone and to let it go. It was over. Lori did not believe it until see saw him with a new girl on campus. It had been a year and a half, and Richard was now ready to prey on his next victim.

Several years later, Lori is still dating much older powerful men and is still being tossed aside after they have had their fun and found a younger victim to prey upon.

> *"Every woman has at least one man to teach*
> *her what she does not want in life."*
>
> —Marsha Holt

It seems harsh and unfortunate, but the saying is true: "Fool me once, shame on you; fool me twice, shame on me." We must at some point make decisions that don't feel good but are right for us. We know when we are about to be sucker punched if it has happened to us before, but for some of us, we rely on the disappointment and the initial hit instead of making the changes needed to ensure us of a different result.

Lori decided to stay in the negative and unfulfilling life she had already grown accustomed to. She was unwilling to be alone and repair the damages from her previous relationship. This kind of decision will deter her from healing and possible future growth. In order to move forward, we must first deal with the current situation and assess how we contributed to it. When will you decide to be in control of your future and not hurt in that way ever again? This is not easy to conceptualize at first, but *you* make the decision of who to love first and more. This person should always, of course, be you.

The confidence you gain once you make this declaration for the first time is indescribable. It is an awakening unlike any other because you have won one of the most important wars you will encounter; you have mastered the art of standing on your own two feet, all alone, because of self-love. This is a joyous time, not a sad one. Yes, you may have lost at love, but you have gained the love and respect of self, and that is so much more important and necessary to experience, obtain, and relish in.

Wendy was thirty-three years old when she left Charles, her abusive boyfriend of five long painstaking years. Her love story was much like everyone else's: they met and fell madly in love. She was just finishing up as a top colorist with one of the top salons in her city and was about to open up her own hair salon when she was first introduced to Charles, a commercial contractor.

Wendy needed help designing her new shop and found him from a valued client. The first year was legendary: they talked, danced, vacationed, spent holidays together, and the sex was unlike anything Wendy had ever encountered. She hoped and prayed that he was the one. The only problem Wendy noticed was his jealous streak that from time to time would rear up its ugly little head.

Charles did not show this side of himself initially, but after the first six months and Wendy's business took off, Charles felt she was at work much too often and not spending enough time with him. He began hanging around the shop more and more and interrogating her about all of her male clients. Wendy first thought it was cute how protective and dedicated he was towards her. She had no idea how bad it was about to become. The first time he lashed out and hit her, he immediately grabbed her close to him and apologized and promised it would never happen again.

Wendy could not believe what had just happened and thought it must have been a mistake on Charles's part. Surely he would never try to hurt his beautiful angel face, as he often referred to her. The hurt and the love she had for this man confused her, and she let him talk his way back in. Before Wendy knew it, she was explaining and making up lies for all of her bruises, black eyes, and sore ribs.

Countless times her friends and family begged her to get out, but she would find some strange reason to stay. She longed for the days when they first met and things were beautiful. Deep down inside, Wendy knew it was no use: it would only get worse. She had lost all respect for Charles, but most of all for herself. She constantly told herself, "You are not this kind of woman." Well, unfortunately, Wendy was just that type of woman; she was abused.

Now Wendy could allow herself to hate Charles and seek revenge, but how much time could she lose in the pursuit of hurting Charles and getting even? Does it make sense to focus on his anger and pain instead of her own? We spend so much time focusing on the wrong things. Wendy needs to find a new set of goals for her future and concentrate only on making them a reality. She will never get her time from Charles back, so why waste more negative energy and time on him?

We have to realize that people usually come into our lives for a reason, but sometimes they come simply because we allowed them to. We have to assume responsibility for our actions and let it go; let go of the hurt, abuse, and self-hate we inflict upon ourselves. Forgiveness is hard, and it is not an innate part of our matrix as human beings. It is an art we must learn to master and control.

The art of forgiveness was preached to me all of my life by my parents, but believe it or not, I too had a very difficult time forgiving my ex-husband and more importantly myself. I wanted to hold onto the anger and pain for far too long. I blamed myself for allowing his abusive nature into my life, and then I blamed him for being the ass I knew he was long before I ever married him. It was a vicious cycle, and it only kept me living in the past. It was as if I needed to still have him around for some ungodly reason.

We can get so caught up in an abusive union that we need help to release it even after the abuse has ended. My momma would say to me, "Do not give that SOB one more day of your thoughts, joy, or tears." She urged me to no longer live in the past and give him the permission to hurt me any longer. My mother preached and pleaded with me for the first two years after my divorce, and even now I ask her to keep me straight when things with my ex go wrong and I slip back into my old ways of thinking and feeling.

We need to have a person we can go to that will help us regroup and remain sane during our times of relapse. It is important to have people close to us who will encourage us to keep it together and push through the trying times. Letting go of an old habit is hard, but letting go of an old and abusive relationship is life altering. Having others to talk to about the abuse provides us with a buffer to relax and release the pain that may emerge from time to time.

Knowing there are others who have experienced this defeat can be helpful. There are many ways to vent and find solace from failed relationships. Individual therapy may be best for any of you who are dealing with shame and/or shyness. Group counseling or joining organizations for survivors of abuse is another excellent way to turn pain into triumph. Abusive relationships can cause self-doubt, worry, wrinkles, diseases, and even death. Whatever you are experiencing, please find the refuge you need.

Ladies, we have to love ourselves enough to fight through these times and move on. Aretha Franklin said it best in one of her songs.

She sang, "I'll be fine even if I have to fake it." That's right, Aretha: fake it until you can make it. I fooled many friends, even my mother, when I was plotting to leave my husband. Friends would call me and spill their guts about their hurtful relationships and how they too were contemplating divorce, but I remained silent because I knew I was no longer talking, I was walking out and walking out soon. I had suffered long enough and knew that this time I would have to choose *my* happiness first.

I realized I had to do this if my girls were ever going to see a whole happy mother (woman) whom they could identify with and later emulate. The real truth in all this is, we need to be there for ourselves, but we also need to be there for others. Learning to forgive and taking hold of the gift of life given to us is a lesson that will bless ourselves and others.

There is always someone watching how you handle and conquer troubles within your life. The outcomes, good or bad, are always being evaluated by some troubled or needful person around you. Ultimately your victories are oftentimes strength for others to draw upon to aid them while they too are struggling. I was banking on one day being happy and fulfilled to the point my children would never ever remember the lonely, saddened, afraid, mistreated, and insecure woman that had been their mother.

My children had to see a woman who was empowered and self-assured. There was no way that could happen if I remained in a union where I was constantly begging to be heard, loved, and recognized as the phenomenal woman I was. We all are amazing creatures just to be here making an effort to love and cultivate a life with anyone—man, children, or coworkers. We often lose ourselves in the rut of everyday living.

It takes a lot of spirit to get up day in and day out trying to make a life for our families. Let's not even talk about how most of us are trying to make some of these people happy as well. The most important person in the world is you! My amazing mother used to tell me all the time, "If you put others before you, who is going to see about you and your needs?" Bitterness and rage begin when we lose ourselves in the sea of making others our priority.

We tend to do things for others thinking it will be appreciated, reciprocated, and at the very least remembered. Well, ladies, do know this: if and when you put someone else before your own needs and wants, it needs to be done from the heart. Unfortunately, just because you love a person in a certain way—selflessly, completely, and forever—does not mean they will return love the same way. We are individuals, and that means we will love that way too. I am a very emotional and affectionate person. I love to kiss, hug, and show how I feel about a person. My children are smothered with hugs and kisses.

The men in my life have all said at one time or another, "You are so emotional" or "You are so affectionate." Well, that is me in all my glory. However, for me to expect them to reciprocate these gestures of love in the very same manner is foolish. Unfortunately, ladies, for many years I did just that. I tried to make the people in my life love me in the manner in which I loved them. In most situations, this will not happen.

It is hard to let things go when we have lived with them for such a long time. I know from my own experiences how people learn to live with pain and oftentimes rely on it to survive. It takes practice, power, and strength to forgive and forget past pains and mistakes we allowed into our lives. I am still relying on certain friends and family members to keep me straight when I try to relapse into counterproductive behaviors.

We all at some time or another wish for love or companionship so desperately that we make foolish decisions. However, the way to break this habit is first by forgiving ourselves for being impatient in love, and secondly, by remembering the long suffering we experienced from our past desperate acts. By consistently focusing on what is good and appropriate for our lives, we allow time and careful decision making to keep us on the right track.

You have to allow people to be who they are. Trying to manipulate people to love you is another way bitterness sets in. You know the man you're with cannot give you what you need, but yet you keep trying to prove yourself and him wrong. This is crazy! Why are you wasting so much of his and your time? Let it go, and let bygones be bygones.

RECAP OF CHAPTER 7

1. Life is full of curve balls; learn to go with the flow.

2. Some things just are not meant to be; let go of whatever is holding you back from your future.

3. Stop trying to control the love process. It has its own time frame and its own agenda. Merely enjoy the ride.

4. *Forgive* the man who cannot love you the way you love him. It is what it is.

5. Stop wasting your time on what you know is not for you.

Chapter 8
Treat a Man Like A Man

In the words of Prince, the musical artist, "Let a woman be a woman and a man be a man." We (women) are evolving every day in this country by leaps and bounds. Consequently, as this process of change manifests, men are also changing. It is not possible to change a mode of operations and not have any of the affiliates change as well. We are no longer one thing or the other. We are usually mothers, career women, and wives. This occurrence has in many instances changed our counterparts (men) as well.

There was a time when a man knew he would make the money and be the only provider for his household. He knew his wife would raise the children and run a tight ship at home. He was assured that she would always be there to take care of things, ready and waiting for him to come home to her once he was finished with his day of slaying the big bad dragon. There was a time when men even thought they were smarter than women. Many of them still believe that crap, but it used to be an unstated reality for society as a whole.

Well, what in the world has happened? We have become educated and not just in academia but in work, money, sports, and even in men.

We now know what we want in and out of the bedroom, and we have even become comfortable in expressing these needs and desires to our men. Many of us have become so comfortable within our new freedom and skin that we now are demanding of our families, jobs, and society as a whole what we expect and need. All of these things are beautiful; however, what have we done to our counterparts in the process of self-evolving the female race?

Many of us fail to see how our evolution has changed the men in our lives. Adding insult to injury, some of this confusion between the sexes is our fault. We have in some situations made our men weak, lazy, and indifferent to us. We believe we can do it all, and I have seen some women who do, but we have also excused our men from their responsibilities as men. There has to be balance in our lives in order for us to feel appreciated and respected by men.

There has to be a fluid exchange of respect and admiration between man and woman in order for us to live together cohesively. We have become more like men in the pursuit of being Super Woman. I have made this mistake, and now I have finally come to an understanding of how we often get in our own way. The following example illustrates a woman losing control because there is no balance in her marriage.

Jessica is a thirty-three-year-old divorced mother of two girls. Her life is hard: she is in school earning her master's degree, working two jobs to make ends meet, and in constant battle with her ex-husband. Jessica's mother has told her repeatedly to stop arguing with Jared and find a middle ground to work out their issues. Jessica is so angry with Jared for losing his job and putting them in financial and emotional turmoil. She has had to be the stronger of the two from the very beginning of the marriage.

Jared is a musician and told Jessica when they were dating that he would never work a regular nine to five job and that she should never ask him to because he wouldn't. Jessica, of course, was in love and did not listen to what Jared was telling her, and at the time Jared was doing great in his career as a studio musician. Life blessed them with two kids and a huge mortgage they could barely make each month.

Jessica kept her needs and desires silent in the hopes that Jared would suddenly see what she was doing and man-up. Year after year came, and nothing changed. Jared remained the same daydreaming, stagnant, and unfulfilled boy he was when he met Jessica. Jessica knew she had made her bed and might very well die in it if she did not try something different. Jessica decided to try life without Jared. She wanted a legal separation in order to sort out her true feelings and see if her life would change. To her surprise, her life did change, and it changed for the better.

We spend so much time hoping things will get better, and they rarely do. There is a part in all of us that wants to be in love and feel special to a man, but we refuse to allow our men in some cases to be just that—men. We want the attention from them so badly we fail to see the man standing before us. I have heard women say, "He is so attractive; we've just got to get him a better job." Another one I've heard too many times is, "Girl, the sex is great; I just wish he'd take me out on a real date sometimes."

It seems we are forever trying to patch us together a whole man. We take bits and pieces of little boys or worse, thugs, and try to make a man that resembles what we really want. This is ludicrous! Let a man be who he is and stop trying to turn him into what you'd have him be. It is so simple, but we have somehow made it difficult and hard to understand.

Men are all around us, but if we are not open to different ideas and possibilities, then we are doomed from the start. Stop taking the leftovers from other women and stop playing Mr. Makeover. Know what a real man is to you first and then wait until he finds you. That's right, I said it, ladies, and I hope you are aware of what I am trying to illustrate.

Men are by nature hunters, and we are in many cases their prey.

Once a man has figured you out, does his attention, patience, and adoration dwindle? Do you find yourself wondering what has happened and why he is no longer calling, chasing, or courting you? Well, the answer is simple: we are doing a few things wrong. We have a tendency to be too easy and too available after we have decided to let him in.

We make the decision to go out with, sleep with, and ultimately marry him. So why do so many of us find ourselves questioning the decisions we thought were right? Could it be we turned over our power to him and became his victim or conquest? Could it be we became so enthralled in him that we lost ourselves and all of our splendor? Could it be we forgot what we wanted and only focused on his needs and dreams? Well, think to yourselves, ladies: who wants to be with a person who has no drive, no dreams, and no decisions of their own to pursue? Men like to focus on us because we are their prey, so why not indulge him in the hunt? Stop giving so much of yourselves too soon.

Men need to chase us, and we need to govern the games that we allow them to play. Take the control back and make him be a man. If he wants to have you, then he must first show he is worthy to have you. Giving him money, clothes, job opportunities, and vacations is no way to land a man. We must stop helping boys become men. The only man a woman should raise is her son. If a man is willing to let you help him financially by giving him money or providing a place for him to eat and live, then he is a boy, not a man, and you do not need him. If you can take care of yourself, then why can't he?

Women are becoming too desperate to have a man. I know all too well because I, too, broke this cardinal rule. I tried to raise my ex-husband. I basically forced him to marry me. I pushed and pushed until I pushed him into something he was not mature enough for. I was ready to take on the world, but he was not in the place I was at that time. He was afraid of losing me, so he popped the question because I basically told him that if we did not get married, then I would begin to date other men and move on. It was terribly wrong of me because he clearly was not marriage material. He was still living at home and did not even have his own car.

I supplied everything for our cheap little existence. I had the car, and I went out and found our apartment. I acted as if I was the man and he was my bride-to-be. It did not dawn on me until much later in life that the marriage was something I and I alone wanted. He only went with it because he was scared and had no other real opportunities.

What was scary about all of this was how desperate and hard-up I was for his time, attention, and strained love.

I was willing to do almost anything to keep him happy and, of course, by my side. It never occurred to me to be free and enjoy my youthful twenties. All I could see was a guy with a little potential and no interest in tapping into it. I did what many of us do—I settled. I settled for a boy instead of a man. I settled for a roommate instead of a husband. I settled for apology after apology instead of true commitment.

The only thing that mattered to me was to have him in my life, instead of waiting for the gentleman I deserved. We cannot know who that gentleman is if we are not aware of who we are and what we need. I had not a clue as to who I was or my potential. All I could see was a possible future with him. The next example will illustrate how women assume that taking care of a man will keep him around.

Sandy was a well-established self-sufficient woman in her late twenties. She had earned her dream career and was now ready for love and commitment. Keith had been on track with his career for a while; however, he was not sure he enjoyed his current lifestyle and was weighing his options as a thirty-three-year-old accountant. He was tired of his mundane existence and needed something different. He wasn't quite sure what he needed; he only knew he could no longer continue on with his present living arrangement.

Keith worked hard in his twenties and had saved a few dollars. He moved out from his parents' home when he left for college but was now in the process of paying off student loans and taking care of himself. Keith decided right before meeting Sandy that he was going to move back in with his parents and take some time off to clear his head. He missed being young and carefree. It was obvious the two were in different places in their lives when they met.

Sandy fell hard and fast for Keith's wittiness and carefree mentality. She began to envision a future for them. She pressured him to move in with her. She was fully aware of his plan to be job free and to not spend his savings, so she basically took care of Keith while he remained on sabbatical.

Sandy cooked, cleaned, paid the bills, and even bought his clothing. She was sure this would keep Keith in her life and possibly one day he would propose. Well, Keith eventually went back to work and immediately met someone new. He left Sandy for Kelly, his office administrator, and married her within one year of meeting her.

"Raising a man to be your man is not supposed to happen."

—Carol Veneables

I know of a few women who have raised strong and powerful daughters but are spoiling and ruining their sons. These women have been hurt and heartbroken by men so badly they subconsciously decide to give their love and attention to their sons. They cook, clean, buy gifts for, and give money to their boys in the hopes they will not leave momma. Karen in the following example gives her all to her son in the hopes he will stay home with her while attending college.

Karen is a forty-year-old mother of two. She has worked hard to keep her kids in good schools and in the best social settings possible. Karen's daughter Nyla is now fifteen years old and is known as momma's personal assistant. Karen's son Mikele is sixteen and is not interested in getting his first job or even passing his driving test. Karen makes Nyla cook and clean up the house, while Mikele idly sits around playing video games and *hanging out with his boyz. No matter what Mikele does, Karen praises him and tells him how attractive he is and how no girl will ever be good enough for her son.*

Nyla is an honor student and is already taking advanced college prep courses in school. She is in several academic and social organizations, and she has taken ballet for close to ten years. Karen loves her daughter and tells her often that she is proud, but she is much harder on and expects more from Nyla than Mikele. Karen has even told Nyla she will have to attend school out of town to help her become more independent but has told Mikele he can stay as close to home as possible (because she will always need a man around to cook and clean for).

Nyla often speaks of the favoritism and lack of equality in the home, but Karen disagrees and explains that Mikele is the man of the house and needs to be treated like the "king" he is. She has even gone so far as to say that if he ever finds a woman as good to him as his momma, he better thank his God first.

This is an excellent example of how we perpetuate an unhealthy situation. Many of us have turned our love for a man over to the love of our sons. We spoil them and make them no good for any woman to call her husband or man. We give attention, money, and adoration to our boys and then expect them to grow up and be men. This habit cripples our boys and keeps them from being men. We are raising our girls but enabling our boys to be selfish, worthless, and childlike men.

In order for anything to grow and be productive, it has to have love, structure, discipline, and a role model to learn from. A single mother has her work cut out for her, but does she want her son to emulate the man who walked out on her, or the man she still dreams of having? A boy will never know how to be a man if you are doing everything for him and never expecting anything in return. You are only making it possible for him to be another useless, using heartbreaker.

Wake up, ladies, and make things different starting in your very own home. Give him expectations to live by and consequences if he fails. Let him know that in order to get anything from a lady, he must first treat and protect her as the lady she is. Make him morally stronger than the men of today and more resilient than the fathers from our pasts. This is not an easy task, but it is a necessity. Who is more equipped to show a boy how to treat and love a woman than his mother? So raise him to adore, respect, and protect the women God has blessed him with.

Another important fact to face is that he can never be the man of your dreams. Your son can never fill the shoes of the man who left or the man you have fantasized about. Yes, he is your little man, but he cannot ever bestow you with the love, intimacy, and respect you need from a man. So stop sitting on the sidelines with your son while safely watching the game of life. Get up off your backside and begin to live as the woman you are now proud of and in love with.

Ladies, please remember that if we have to buy love, then we probably did not have love from the start. Please set the standard for the men in your life and make them live up to it. We have to stop being so desperate, anxious, and ready to accept whatever a man has to offer. If we know who we are and what we want, shouldn't we know what man best befits us as well? Love your life with or without a man and please wait for the right one to show up. Having to create the man of your dreams never works. Let him find you.

RECAP OF CHAPTER 8

1. Live life to your fullest, whether or not a man is a part of it.

2. Allow the man in your life to be a man.

3. Stop making excuses for the man in your life. You cannot change or fix him.

4. Know what you want from a relationship and stop settling.

5. Let the man of your dreams find you. Stop searching for Mr. Right.

Chapter 9
There Are No Victims, Only Volunteers

In the previous chapters, I have stated some of my past pains and mistakes that have led me to writing this book. This chapter covers a major theme in my personal journey toward healing. Throughout most of our lives, we spend too much time blaming others for our hurts and sorrows, when in actuality we are the culprits that need to be confronted.

We all have choices to make. We can choose to be happy or sad. We can choose to be pitied or revered. The ultimate decision rests on our very own shoulders. One of the pitfalls to healing and letting go of the mistakes or the person we made these mistakes with is to blame others. I know all too well about the blame game.

In order for me to feel good or better about my problems, I had to insult, blame, or hate the person I believed caused me to feel this ugly and low within myself. It did not register to me that I was the poor soul who needed to be confronted. I remained in warrior mode because it kept some fraction of the connection with the past, the pain, and the other person. Letting go of anger and hurt meant letting go. I was not ready to do that, so I just held onto what I had left.

My marriage was a joke at its best, and I still tried to hang in there. It did not matter if it was good or bad, as long as it was there. I was comfortable with the pain and disappointments. Most people cannot make changes if they are too comfortable with their situation. Life usually has to place you in an uncomfortable setting in order for you to even seek after change. The next example demonstrates how women accept things when they are in comfortable relationships.

Angela was a strong decisive young woman. At thirty-three years of age, she was a senior executive at a very prestigious software company and had several pieces of property throughout the southeastern area of the United States. Angela grew up watching her mother and father fight over her mother wanting to work and be somewhat independent of her father.

She vowed to never be involved with a man who was competitive with her or a man who was threatened by her accomplishments. Funny how we sometimes set ourselves up for what we say we will never do. Angela became friends and eventually lovers with one of her coworkers, Michael.

They had so much in common. He was athletic and loved to travel just as much as Angela, and he had no prior relationship baggage. He enjoyed being single and had no children. Angela felt he was a little cocky, but she thought that was part of his charm as being one of the top sales execs at work.

Michael's arrogance annoyed her at times, but she had so much fun with him and could really relate to him on so many different levels. Angela found herself making excuses for his cockiness and even began telling herself it was kind of cute. Eventually the day came when she and he had to work on an assignment together and present the project to their superiors. Everything was going fine until the Q&A portion of the meeting began. One of the VPs decided to interrogate a little further than the others because he was not yet sold on their presentation.

Instead of being the professional that Angela was, Michael began placing blame on Angela and even went so far as to explain that he too had issues with some of her ideas and marketing strategies. Angela was embarrassed and humiliated but managed to hold herself together until after the meeting.

After the meeting, she immediately broke things off with him. For several months, Angela blamed Michael for her embarrassment and loneliness. It was not until she had an old recurring dream of watching her parents fight that Angela accepted her part in her pain. She knew Michael could only do what she had allowed him to.

My father used to say to me all the time when I was a schoolgirl, "If it walks like a duck and talks like a duck, then guess what? It probably is one." Michael showed who he was from the very start. Angela chose to ignore it or rationalize it. If we are observant enough, we can avoid making many mistakes.

Many times we talk ourselves right into the very things we know we do not want. I have seen so many people willfully walk themselves right into a miserable marriage and worrisome relationship just in fear of being alone or bored. It is unbelievable to me how successful we are as women and yet we continue to make poor relationship choices. We make decisions out of desperation and fear. We make up goals for ourselves and push on through life and relationships until we obtain them. Many of us marry because of a goal that we are seeking rather than it being a choice made from the heart.

Marriage for men is a choice, rather than a goal that they have set for themselves earlier in life. They typically find "the woman" and then decide to marry. I have heard several men tell me that they had no intention to ever marry but then they met Ms. Right. Women, on the other hand, begin formulating their futures long before Mr. Right ever gets here.

I see all too well right now in my two young daughters how they are planning to get married and start a family before starting a life of their own. I constantly try to instill in them that they need to know who they are before planning their futures with someone else and becoming someone else's mother. I want them to understand how life can be what they dream of if they could just slow down and let it happen.

We set ourselves up to be victims before the game even begins. Society has programmed us to be of service to others before we are of service to ourselves. We hear the quotes "Boys will be boys" and "You can't stop a man from being a man." We also hear "A good woman would stand by her man or know how to handle the man she is with."

These notions have led us into a society where we think that we can change a man or that we should accept when we have selected a mate poorly. We choose who we allow into our hearts and world. We make the decisions for our lives; no one else does.

No one told me to marry my husband but me. I did that all on my own. It was left up to me to save myself and restore my future to the state I wanted it to be. I made it through the fire; it was now time to put out the fire. In order to put out the fire, one must stop holding onto the pain, sadness, indifference, and rage we usually enjoy carrying around.

Now you may be saying to yourself, "I don't enjoy feeling like this." Well, honey, a wise man used to tell me often, "You must like what you're doing because you keep on doing it." If you're doing something over and over again that does not feel good to you and you are not enjoying it, then why do you keep on doing it? Some say we do things out of habit, and some say we do things because we do not know any better.

Well, to me, if you keep practicing at something that makes you feel bad or unfulfilled, then you are an idiot. Hear me out, ladies. I was just that, an idiot. So if I can call myself that, you know what I will call you. Stupid. You are silly and stupid if you keep allowing anyone to make you feel inferior, ugly, not good enough, sad, angry, or enraged.

Life is short, and the only person who can pick up the pieces and move on to greener pastures is you.

Learn this lesson fast, and your life will be productive, inspired, and most importantly, yours. Stop relinquishing your life to the hands of an unworthy mate or dream stealer. Learn to love yourself with all of your flaws so no one, not even your own mother, can sway you away from your happiness and destiny. This may take time and courage to do, but it has to be done.

One way I learned to love myself was by first being okay with being alone. Many of us are never truly alone. We spend so much of our time with others. We work, hang out with friends, take care of our families, and at night many of us go to bed with our husbands, kids, or significant others.

Being alone to listen to your thoughts and dreams is so vital to the human spirit. We live in a world where there is so much noise and stimulus that we can no longer hear ourselves or our feelings. We all need time to be alone and be at peace with it.

It has taken me thirty years to become okay with being alone in my own space. Now there are many of you who are already okay with this. However, for many of us, the thought of having no friends or partner in our lives scares the crap out of us. What will I do with myself? How will I spend my time? What will others think of me if I have no date or nothing to do?

My point in time spent alone is this: How can you know yourself and love the life and skin you're in if you do not have an intimate relationship with yourself? My concern is with young women who are afraid of themselves and their potential to the point of hiding or focusing on others so they will not have to face themselves.

I have done this, and still I find myself at times not spending enough time alone with just Torre. I have had friendships that have kept me from finding me. I have had relationships where I focused so much on him, I could not hear, see, or feel me. This is how we hide from ourselves.

I had to teach myself to place my needs at the top of my priorities list. Many of us struggle with looking out for number one; however, this is the first real step toward self-love. There is a passage I read whenever I feel myself sinking back into my old self-destructive habits:

"Our deepest fear is not that we are inadequate. Our deepest fear is that we are powerful beyond measure. It is our light, not our darkness that most frightens us. We ask ourselves, who am I to be brilliant, gorgeous, talented, and fabulous? Actually, who are you not to be? You are a child of God. Your playing small does not serve the world. There is nothing enlightened about shrinking so that other people won't feel insecure around you. We are all meant to shine, as children do. We are born to make manifest the glory of God that is within us. It's not just in some of us; it's in everyone. And as we let our own light shine, we unconsciously give other people permission to do the same. As we are liberated from our own fear, our presence automatically liberates others."

—*Marianne Williamson*

This statement has helped me see that I am supposed to be in control of my life, my happiness, my health, my wealth, my relationships, and the people whom I allow into my world. It is when I allow someone else's power of self to overshadow or overpower my own that I become fearful and a victim. Learn to let your light shine, and let it shine so brightly that it encourages others to do the very same.

We have to sometimes get away from others in order to do what is necessary for us to love ourselves. Reading this passage gives me the confidence to be who I am and to not fear the splendid blessings that are waiting for me out there in the universe. It assures me that God did not make a mistake when he created me and that every one of us is here for a purpose. This passage encourages me to remove the fear from my being.

Fear is not of us, it is of hell. It is a tool used on this earth to keep great things from happening. When we turn ourselves over to it, it can and will wreak havoc over our lives, families, and futures. Where there is fear, there is insecurity, jealousy, envy, self-doubt, sadness, shame, hurt, destruction, and of course pain. Stop being a victim. Stop making excuses for others, and learn to stand on your own and love yourself even when others claim that you are not worthy of it. Learn to forgive your past mistakes and move on from it. Do not remain there another moment. Forgiveness of others is a must for us to progress, but it is imperative to also learn to forgive yourself.

Recap of Chapter 9

1. Learn to let fear go. Practice every day by focusing on perfect and positive thoughts.

2. *Forgiveness of self and others is a must,*

3. Stop being a victim.

4. Love yourself even when others say you are not deserving of it.

5. Stop making excuses to hide your shining light. Be a bright shooting star.

Knowledge and Wisdom

"Happy is the person who finds wisdom and gains understanding."

—Proverbs 3:13

We have come to the place where we have survived our battles, and now we are feeling empowered and ready to share our victories. This is the process of growth and progress. We should first learn for ourselves how to love ourselves and then share that accomplishment with others who are also treading down that weathered road. This happiness you are feeling needs to be shared and witnessed by others who are trying to get to the peaceful place you now reside in.

Chapter 10
Friends or Foes

Now you are beginning to find your voice and spirit, and it seems others are wrecking your flow. This is unfortunate but natural as well. People have a tendency to accept and parade you when you are miserable and downtrodden. It is sad to say but true, misery does love company.

Many of us can only be comfortable with others when they too are lonely, broke, in a bad relationship, or just not truly fulfilled in life. Have you ever noticed how a good friend or even boyfriend will frown upon changes you have integrated into your life? For example, you decide to go back to school or start a new career field. There are those who cheer you on. They tell you it is a great move to make and wish you well. Then there are those who find as many reasons as possible for you not to pursue your dreams.

Well, this chapter is dedicated to what I call the dream haters—the people in our lives who try to put us in a box and dare us not to move out of it. They come in many disguises. There are the ones who tell you upfront that you are stupid, weak, broke, or too ugly to accomplish your dreams. They love to capitalize on your shortcomings and tell you every chance they get. Then there are the ones who appear to be in agreement with you, but deep down they are hoping and praying you will not make it because then they will feel even more of a failure than they already do. These people are usually family and friends, because who else do we listen to and respect as much as these people?

It is sad to say, but most of the dream haters are family and they know exactly how to dampen our spirits and place shadows over our dreams and aspirations. We go to them to bounce around ideas and to share an accomplishment we made. However, we leave their presence feeling doubtful, insecure, and sometimes even afraid of what we had set out for ourselves to do.

An old wise woman once told me to be careful who you share your dreams with because just as you pray to succeed, they can pray against you in hopes you fail. Well, I agree with the fact that people will try to sabotage your agendas and ideas, but I also disagree with anyone having the power to hinder or stop you from what is already yours. When we dream and set out to obtain those dreams, they are ours to begin with and ours to the completion. No one, and I mean no one, can stop what is yours to begin with. The following example will illustrate this point.

Nona was a slacker as a kid. She never really liked school and made average grades. Her parents would ride her all the time about being more assertive and ambitious in life. Nona found herself never measuring up to her parents' expectations and wishing she could find something she was interested in.

Finally one day Nona began taking a class in sewing as a way to learn how to make all of the cool clothes she saw in the malls and on T.V. Suddenly it all began to make sense, and Nona realized she wanted to become a fashion designer. She took course after course and breezed through them effortlessly. Her parents were amazed at the change in her.

Nona went from sleeping in late on the weekends and needing prodding to do her chores to getting up early in the morning, exercising, and even learning how to cook for her parents. She had a new love for life that she had never felt before. Her boyfriend of two years, Zack, was not too thrilled with all of the changes.

Zack was a slacker, too, and was very threatened by all of Nona's newfound ambition. He teased her about her dreams of becoming a top clothing designer and told her it was stupid to exercise as much as she was because he could not see any changes in her at all from it. His insecurities turned his teasing into verbal abuse.

Nona began to feel drained when she was around Zach. Whenever she thought about showing him her work, she felt anxious and nervous. Nona felt betrayed and hurt by Zack's abuse, to the point she no longer shared her life or her accomplishments with him. She slowly started to pull away from him completely. Zack tried to keep his foot in the door of Nona's life, but Nona was alive and excited about her new life. She wanted only to be supported and validated by the people who claimed to love her.

"No matter how many people try to sabotage you, keep on going."
—Maureen Cahill

This is an example of how people can place us in a box and dare us not to move or climb out of it. It is as if our staying in that box defines to them who they are. They have no belief or imagination of ever seeing their dreams becoming a reality.

It never even dawns on them that we, too, have dreams and agendas of our own. No matter where we go in life, we will find these types of people because the average person has issues with jealousy, envy, insecurities, and fear. We all at some time or another fear that someone will be more accomplished, educated, successful, and/or powerful than us. It is natural to have these feelings. However, how we handle these emotions or the people who treat us poorly because of these emotions is crucial to our overall well-being.

Nona could have allowed Zack to remain in her life and wreak havoc over her. She could have also challenged him to get up off his rear end and find his gift in life as well. We all have a gift that only we can possess and embrace as our mission in life. The key to this mission is knowing yourself well enough to trust your voice and find that gift that belongs to you and only you.

It took me some time to figure out that I had real friends and what I call wannabe friends. They were the ones who loved to see me dream big but fall flat on my face in pursuit of my dreams every once in awhile. In order for them to be okay in their box, they had to see me stay inside of mine. If I dared try to climb out, they would always suggest I see the whole picture before trying something new.

I heard all sorts of comments in regard to certain agendas I made for my life. "What do you mean you're going to Europe with your new husband to try out his musical career? What about your family here in the states; you could just pack up and leave them?" Never thinking of me or my new future with my husband, all they could see was from where they were standing.

I had a friend who decided since I married, she no longer had anything in common with me. Funny how some friendships can only go so far or remain for so long. In some ways I feel they are not true friends, just people placed in our lives to show us who we really are. They allow us to see how we handle life in the presence of others.   Have you ever noticed how the quality of a friendship can be determined by some women in regard to whether or not they have a man in their life? God forbid if you have a man, and these same women do not. When they have a mate or partner, they hardly call you and will cancel a date with you in a minute if he calls. While if you have the man, then they are quick to say, "Let's do something—just us, no men." They love to tell you that they cannot be the third wheel going out or that they feel uncomfortable being the only single person there.

These types of insecurities used to drive me crazy with one of my old girlfriends. No matter how often I would try to include her with me and my significant other, if she was not seeing someone, she would refuse to go out with us. I thought this was a little insecure of her and continued to invite her out with us regardless of her constant refusals. I don't care if you have two dates and I have none; if I am your friend and enjoy your company, I am very comfortable in being alone among couples.

We women have got to stop placing so much weight and importance on being in a relationship and having a man. There are going to be many instances in life when we are alone and, honey, get used to it. If I have no friends or significant other in my life, I am happy and at peace with being just plan ole me.

It took me years to get to this place, but let me tell you, the peace that comes with being your own best friend and companion is unbelievable. For many of my adult years, my mother would encourage me to be alone and listen to my inner voice, but I was too afraid of myself and too frantic with life to sit still and be at ease with the voice that resonates inside of me.

This voice is in each of us, and it allows us to find peace and solace from within ourselves. It is how we feed ourselves from within emotionally. Life today, however, has become so hectic and fast paced that we no longer have the time or fortitude to seek this vital place of refuge. In the days of old, we had no choice but to hear ourselves think; without consistent stimulus, women had to hear themselves think, reason, and yes, reflect over their attempts at making their lives whole and fulfilled.

It was easier to see people for who they were, and it was easier to understand who we were. Now we have so many others trying to tell us who we should be that we live in a perpetual state of conflict. A girl has so many resources to tell her she is inadequate. There are a plethora of resources to choose from: the haters, magazines, television, Internet, and radio all keeping us in a virtual state of visual stimuli on what and how we can be what others think we should be.

Learning to be at peace within comes from listening to within. What do you hear even when you think life is at its best? What do you hear when you know that you know that a particular person is no good for your life? These gut-wrenching notions and thoughts are the ones we miss out on if we are not on point from within. If we have not trained ourselves how to be still and listen to the sounds of our souls, we often miss out on signs and signals of trouble ahead of us.

I was so screwed up during my tumultuous marriage that I could not sleep at night. I would hear my soul speaking out at night, and it was telling me how miserable I was and how life should not be the way it was. I found myself praying all hours of the night just so I could fall off to sleep. Eventually I gained the courage and the sense to listen to my inner voice and make some changes in my life.

Now that we have discussed becoming at peace with how splendid we are, let's also remember we are here to inspire and aid others who have fallen victim to the manner in which we used to be held captive. Ladies, do not be afraid to share your pains, hurts, and disappointments with other ladies who are lost but looking to find their way past the pain. We all need an encouraging word, helping hand, and a slap on the behind when we are trudging through whatever test God has placed before us. So keep your head up and please keep going, whether or not there is a friend or a man to see you through. You will get there, and you will conquer whatever is in front of you if and only if you choose to.

RECAP OF CHAPTER *10*

1. Venture out and enjoy being your own best friend. You may learn something new about you.

2. Stop allowing others to determine when and where you will have a good time. It is your journey, no one else's.

3. Every day of your life, be grateful for you and what you possess.

4. People will disappoint you and fail you; that's just life.

5. Learn that each day is a day to become wiser and more knowledgeable of your desires, passions, and goals.

Chapter 11
The Love of a Good Man Begins Inside of You

We are now happy with our lives and okay with being alone. We would like a hot and passionate relationship with a deserving man, but if he is not here yet, we are just fine with that as well. Well, here he comes when we are not even thinking about him. What do we do now that he has swept us off of our very stable and balanced feet?

First we thank God for spicing up our lives with a noteworthy companion, and we also need to *learn* how to let someone love us. This has been a hard lesson for me. I spent the majority of my adult life being disappointed and abused until I thought I should look for trouble and, of course, expect it. It has been a hard pill to swallow, but yes, I do now know that in order to receive love you must first believe you deserve it and ultimately know how to return the loving as well.

We wait and wait and wait for real love and learn from all of the trial and error that comes with it. What happens when it is really here? What is a scared, fractured girl to do? I have heard my father and stepmother tell me over and over again, "It is okay to let someone love you. You are a great girl, you deserve this, let it happen, stop trying to manipulate it." It took me a while to relax and allow this awesome man to come into my life and make my life a little easier for me.

It is weird being in a relationship where someone else is doing most of the pursuing and chasing. It at first did not feel natural at all. I thought I always had to do something for him or give to him first in order for him to give to me. Well, he has taught me what a real man looks, acts, sounds, and feels like.

He has taught me that the man in your life should love, respect, honor, protect, and cherish your heart and soul. He has shown me true friendship and decency. Many men today are far removed from being decent. We women have become accustomed to men catcalling, cursing, hitting, yelling, and publicly embarrassing us. Many of us do not even realize a man should never disrespect you. He should never treat you anything less than the lady you are.

Ladies, when the love of a good man comes along, I hope you are ready in all areas to receive it. Being in a successful relationship is hard work. You have mastered being in love with yourself; now it is time to let go and let love. Give the man a chance to be the knight in shining armor you've been waiting for.

The next example illustrates how some women refuse to let go and let love lead the way. Natalie has done all of the work to get to this special place in her life. She now needs to loosen up and learn to trust herself in love.

Natalie is a thirty-five-year-old banker and has finally met "the man." He is almost everything she has dreamed of. Natalie usually goes for a tall lean-bodied man. Nate, on the other hand, is a little less tall and a little rounder than Natalie prefers, but she loves Nate all the same for his stable mind, assured loving grasp, and comforting presence.

She knows that he is it! After many trials and errors, she has found her golden guy. Although there is one problem, Natalie is scared to let go and love. She is delighted to find a man who knows how to communicate what he feels and needs. He also knows how to decipher what she needs as well.

The problem is Natalie is comfortable being in control of everything, including her intimate and sexual emotions. She has gotten used to taking "care of herself" sexually and intimately when there is no promise of a man in her life. She enjoys her love life with Nate, but she just cannot seem to let go and surrender herself to him totally.

They have been married now for seven months, and Nate is still trying to pull down the walls that Natalie has so triumphantly put up. Night after night Nate reaffirms his love and commitment to Natalie, but she is reluctant to let him in. He has become frustrated and turned off by the whole thing. His attempts to make love with her are becoming fewer, and Natalie knows she cannot keep holding back from him much longer. She has no clue what to do about this.

This has happened to me, and it is not only frightening but also very difficult to understand and to process through. I thought once I had met the right man, that everything else would come naturally. Wrong! Wrong! Wrong!

We tell ourselves each time there is a new relationship or opportunity to start a new one, that this time things will be different. Well, it takes two people to have a relationship, and it takes two people to screw one up. This means that we have to assume some of the burden of ruining a relationship.

We need to be clear about a few things. Each and every one of us has learned or innately been given detrimental information to a healthy relationship. For me it was fear. I would always expect terrible things to happen long before any sign or symptom appeared of trouble. I always would see the negative before the positive, and I would expect to receive a negative response before a positive one.

This is a lesson I am still working on. I have a very imaginative mind and because of the abuse and pain from my previous relationship,

I all too often feel or think I will be sucker-punched in the gut or disappointed long before anything ever happens.

The man I am seeing has said often that I look for trouble and problems to occur. This looking for flaws and errors in my mate has got to be a turnoff for most men. My boyfriend mentioned when we first began dating from time to time, "Don't make me pay for his mistakes, or better yet, I am not your trouble from your past!"

This can only go on for so long before we have pushed a great guy right from our grasp. Ladies, please be advised if you are not totally in love and assured of who you are and where you are in life, he will pick up on it. Please pray he is a patient and tolerant man who will walk the healing journey with you. There are so many healthy men out there who have no time or need to see you through your healing.

Make sure when the relationship and conversations are heading toward commitment that he is aware of the fact that you are still searching and developing toward your whole and complete self. I am sure most of us know when we are not all there yet and still need a little time. However, life is funny, and he may come into your life before you are at your full potential, so have the conversation with him and let him know how deep your baggage is.

He may surprise you and tell you it is okay and that you are worth the wait, or he may tell you he is not ready to carry or discover new depths of your pains. If it is the latter, then you have confirmation he is not the right guy for where you are at that time. You may need additional alone time to fully recover from all of your baggage.

How Do You Know What Your Baggage Is?

This is an amazing question to some, but still I say, to thy self be true. I think when we are still and quiet within ourselves, we understand or feel what is inhibiting us from peace. Peace is the beginning to knowledge of the self, wisdom of the spirit, and unshakable self-understanding. When I was married, deep down inside I knew I was fearful of my very own potential and scared as hell to be alone.

I knew I needed and wanted more out of life than my ex-husband did, and I also knew he knew it and that is why he tried so diligently to control me. It was so bad that I made excuses and strived for the bare minimum just to stay in line with him and what he wanted. I played myself down and hid my life from my friends and family because I knew they, too, would see through me and urge me to leave him.

Ladies, we fear ourselves because we have no true understanding of just how powerful and special we are. There is absolutely nothing we cannot do once we are aware of how priceless we are. I spent ten years of my life living his dreams and making excuses for his losses.

It was not until I was thirty-four years old that I realized my life and my future rest on my contribution to my well-being and no one else's, It was always up to me, and it usually was my doing that allowed us to have vacations, a clean home, furniture, and anything else I wanted us to have. Once I realized I could exist and do so beautifully without him at all, I began to reinvest in me and start challenging myself to do and want more from life.

Whether you are an addict, financially challenged, sick in spirit or health, there is one thing I know to be fact, until we give those ailments up to God and ask to be fortified by him and through him, we will remain lost and frustrated. There is nothing that my God could not restore in me. When I was scared, he gave me the strength to get up and see another day. When I was alone, he wrapped his holy spirit around me and rocked me to sleep. When I was broke, he found a way to send money to me. I have been divorced for almost five years, and I live, love, and laugh, better and harder now than I ever could have imagined when I was married.

It takes obstacles and strife to prove who and what we are. Just because we have been troubled or flawed does not mean we have to stay in that pain, abandonment, and worriment. Ladies, life is hard; let no one fool you about that. Finding peace and solace in myself through God is the way in which I made it through; to be honest, I think it is the only real way to make it. He has never failed me nor forsaken me.

In my darkest times with myself, he has come to spread light, peace, and love for me to see my way clear of harm's way. *We all have baggage and things we are ashamed of, but loving ourselves even when others don't, letting go of self-hate, and believing things will change when we decide to change them is how to make it through.* I am pretty sure God has allowed this good man into my life. I am not sure how long or why, but I do believe that good things can and will happen to us all if we just simply believe they should.

Give yourself and life a chance to reaffirm your worth to you. My daddy says to me all the time, "Every dog has its day, and if you're a good little dog, you may have two." Well, I believe if we think on goodness, we will receive good things, so expect only good days because we know the bad ones are going to find us somehow.

Learn to laugh and love and not see yourself as the person who once toted so much baggage. Look into your mirror each day and tell yourself just how beautiful, smart, and sexy you are, whether there is love or not in your life.

Know that God made you perfect in your own special way and no other opinion of you matters. If you are blessed with a miraculous love, tell yourself you deserve this love and you know how to receive and return good love. Ladies, we have to live each day as if it was the very last and thank God for a new day full of new chances. Chances are a blessing from God we are given each day. We must learn to utilize these gifts in order to produce the outcomes we are searching for.

The law of attraction and nature illustrates that what we focus on and put out into the universe, we will get back. That is why it feels so good to surprise or help a person in need. We all love to be surprised with gifts, love notes, or thoughtful cards, so when we give these surprises, we are most often smiling because we know how it feels when we are surprised. It is a reciprocal act.

Well, then, focus on goodness and positive things, and surely the exact same thing will come to you. It allows us to be in control of what is coming to us soon. If you know you deserve a good relationship and you are well prepared and ready to receive a good thing, then why would it not find you at some point?

Letting go of the past and preparing yourself for good things each and every day is the start to being healthy and having a healthy relationship with not just a good man but anyone else you encounter as well. There will be all kinds of women and men to enter our lives; some are for a reason, a season, or a lifetime. The choice again rests on you and where you are inside of your personal *unknown woman* development.

Hopefully you now know what you want and how to handle anything or anyone that now enters the door of your world. You are so confident in yourself now that no matter how alone or lonely you may be, you know things will be okay because you are at peace with being just you.

Trusting to Love and Letting Go

There are only a few animals that mate for life. The one animal that intrigues me more than any other is the bald eagle. Now, ladies, this chick has her act together when it comes to the mating game. Here is how it goes. When the female eagle has reached her time to mate and reproduce, she has a ritual she follows in order to select her mate. Now I hope you read when I stated that *she selects him*, not the other way around.

Once she has found a suitable suitor, she flies up really high with a stick in her mouth and drops it. The suitor quickly swoops down to retrieve the stick and offers it to her. She, of course, does not take the stick from him; instead, she flies up even higher with a larger stick and drops it. Each time she flies higher than the last time, and the stick in her mouth gets larger as well.

This courtship could very well kill the suitors that try to pursue her. She tries to make this courtship as difficult as possible for her suitors. This ritual can go on and on and on because most suitors give up and move on. This female eagle is smart, strong, clever, and most of all patient. She knows her mate has to be just as patient, strong, and committed to her as she is to him.

So finally she finds a persistent mate, one that retrieves every stick she rejects, even the biggest stick that almost caused him to swoop down to his very own death. So what does she do next? This chick flies up to a height that she does not usually fly to and falls back down on her back at an enormous deadly speed. The male eagle (her mate now for life) has proven that he is down for whatever she throws his way, so he flies down underneath her and basically balances her with his back to hers as they fly in perfect harmony with one another.

This is probably one of the most profound mating rituals nature has to offer us. Ladies, know yourself so well that you can see what your mate is willing to do for your hand in life. Be courageous enough to make him prove how awesome he is for your life.

Once you know what you are, then and only then can you select a mate who will pursue you like the bald eagle. You know your own strength, your tenacity, and grit. You know what you are made of and how to make things happen for yourself, so don't you dare settle and miss out on your true perfect counterpart. Make him prove how far he is willing to go. Because we all know, *we deserve it.*

> *"You can only change yourself, so do it and*
> *let everything else fall where it may."*
> —Kathan Fillingim

Torre M. Prothro, M.A.

SOME THINGS JUST AIN'T MEANT TO BE

Now you are empowered, strong, and much more fearless of love than before. You have had a few decent relationships, but none have lasted very long. So here you are in what appears to be "the relationship," but it is just a tad bit off. You cannot place your fingers on it, but it does not feel like a perfect fit. He is sweet, thoughtful, loyal, attractive, hardworking, God-fearing, and yes, your family adores him, but somewhere in the pit of your stomach, you hear that new self-assured voice telling you this is not the one. You're scared to hurt his feelings, and you're a little sad of what may be ahead of you, but deep down you know what has to be done.

This is not the first time this kind of thing has happened, and you are now in a place of knowledge and wisdom where you know exactly how to handle this situation. You are now capable of receiving love, and you are also strong enough to be alone and okay about it. There is no other choice to make but to let him go, so you're clear and free for "the one."

Many times we are not okay with being alone. We are too fearful that *the one* may never show up, so we take advantage of this great guy. We use him to remain comfortable and to have a companion in our life. There are some who may even marry him because of the insecurity of being alone or from the pressure of others.

Well, I hope this is not you. Hopefully you have realized who you are and what it takes to make you happy and content with your life. The whole point to this scenario is that you have arrived and settling just won't do. You are now living in your unknown woman's skin, and it feels good. Keep your sights on the sky and enjoy all life has to offer and all you have fought for. Know that whatever you envision for your life, you can make it happen. You now have ownership of your life for whatever does or does not happen. Enjoy it. Protect it. Love fearlessly and from the heart.

Finding someone to love you is a blessing. However, knowing how and when to return love shows growth and maturity. Playing it safe and holding onto a man you are not in love with shows you are not ready to handle the precious gift of love. Sometimes we have to respect the nature of love enough to be completely honest with a person even if it means saying no to what they think is true love. Be prepared to blow a few people's minds with the growth and strength you now possess.

You will be amazed as well when you realize you have learned your true power, mastered your strength, learned to forgive, and now live in a reality of newfound knowledge and wisdom. It is refreshing, ladies, to know just how awesome we are and that we must first fall in love with our whole existence before we expect a man to.

RECAP OF CHAPTER 11

1. The hard work has been done. Loosen up and be easy.

2. You are wise enough now to trust in real love.

3. Let go of your previous baggage and love life exuberantly.

4. Know that with this new wisdom, you may lose supposed friends.

5. Trust in the fact that all you have accomplished *you now deserve.*

Chapter 12
Have You Found Your Unknown Woman?

Once you have the *power,* then you get the *strength*; once you have the strength, then you learn to *forgive;* once you learn to forgive, then and only then will you have *knowledge* that hopefully carries you into divine *wisdom*. I am very hopeful this will allow you some insight into finding and loving the unknown woman within you. Before we began this chat, some of us were afraid of our potential, angry with ourselves and others, victims, and holding onto the past and all the negativity attached to it.

The thought of being okay from within was hard to conceptualize, let alone find peace with. I remember how hard it was for me to look in the mirror and focus on my inner beauty and why I deserved to be truly happy and at peace with my life. For a very long time I did not think that happiness was real. I thought it was something that many women were faking, like me.

There were so many books and magazines out there about loving yourself and falling in love with you, but to me all of this was quite abstract and very difficult to conceive of. Learning to like me was hard enough, but actually falling in love with me did not become a reality until I was well into my thirties. So for all of the late bloomers and younger ladies in your twenties struggling with this love affair, please know that this is a constant effort that has no end. You will forever evolve and grow as you find this *unknown woman* within you.

Once she has been discovered, there is no turning back to the old you. You will begin to understand that life lies in the palm of your hands and there is where you will determine how, when, and where your happiness and pleasure will thrive. From time to time, you might fall back into old habits or ways of thinking, but just remember that it all relies on you.

One day you may have a setback and run into an ex that is doing great and appears to be extremely happy with a new promising love. This may happen after you have experienced another breakup or life may be just a tad bit too heavy. Keep your mind on how far you have come and remember you, too, will be happier again. We must remember if we relinquish our happiness to another person's happiness or failures, then we are once again giving up our control and our power to another person.

It took me awhile to forgive my ex-husband and all of the pain the relationship caused me. It took me even longer to wish him happiness and success in life. Ladies, you know what I am talking about. When relationships fail us, we want the man that caused us this pain to experience pain himself. We want him to hurt and to hurt badly.

Well, this is normal, but at some point you have to let go and move on to more productive thoughts and emotions. We have to understand in order for us to receive love, we must wish love for others. We have to have an unselfish heart and spirit while generating the flow of love. We have to get over the hurt from another person's humanness and truly forgive. Like I stated in previous chapters, what you put out to the universe, you will receive it back. So if you are wishing hardships and pain to a person, you will pull that same experience in to yourself.

Margo and Sam had been married for seven years when Sam decided to have an affair with his new assistant at work. The affair went on for three years before Margo had the slightest clue as to what was going on. This was a bitter pill to swallow for Margo because she had been what she thought to be a perfect wife. She had her own career and was an excellent mother to their five-year-old daughter.

The affair was found out later to be only the tip of the iceberg for Sam's indiscretions. After one year in therapy, Margo learned Sam had always cheated and that it was difficult for him to be monogamous. He finally told her he did not think he could ever be faithful to just one woman.

Being the sophisticated and bright woman Margo is, she decided to end the marriage. Many of their friends sided with her after the divorce and often tried to console Margo. There was no consoling her, though. Margo wanted Sam to hurt as she did, and she constantly thought of the very moment that he would get his.

A few years after the divorce, Margo still hated Sam. She was so hurt and devastated that what she thought would be her happily-ever-after was just the opposite. The pain and revenge she held onto from Sam was now controlling her life. This vengeance began to consume her to the point it made her tired and she began to look aged.

Margo decided to start fresh and try to reassemble her shattered life. She began to date again, and it was no walk in the park for her. She constantly thought how she missed being married and feeling safe and secure. Time eventually changed the hurt into knowledge and wisdom because Margo was beginning to see life for the very first time as hers and hers alone.

She no longer had the picture-perfect thoughts of her future and how it would be. She began to see and understand that her life was a series of decisions, successes, and mistakes. She also realized this was the only way she would learn more about herself.

Eventually she forgave Sam and even learned to accept that if Sam had not done what he did, then she would never have learned exactly what she was made of. Margo even went a step further and wished Sam peace and happiness in his life because Margo also realized that just because Sam could not be the husband she rightfully deserved, he too still deserved to find happiness and lead the life he was entitled to.

Ladies, one thing that came to me while I was going through my divorce was the fact that when love fails us, it is only the beginning to another love story. The first love affair, of course, is reestablishing love from within. This new relationship was hard to establish with myself. However, once I found my footing, everything else fell into place. How can I have the love I deserve if I remain in a troubled, unfulfilling, and insane relationship with myself?

We tend to pull into our lives whatever we focus and rely on to be our truths. If we choose to believe this fact, then life will bring us love if we choose it; but if we choose to only see failure and loss, then—guess what—that is exactly what we will receive.

I knew my ex-husband and I had gone as far as we could possibly go and that time had run out on us. He was not the same man, and I was certainly not the same woman. If I had stayed and continued to live the lie I was living, I would have eventually died from my full potential of becoming me.

Now this may sound mystical or creepy, but I am so happy to have gone through that part of my life and done so at an early age. I am better in all realms of my life because of my failed marriage. I also think of how better off my ex-husband must be to be free to be who he truly is without having to hide and lie about himself anymore. We often as women only see our hurt and our failures. We do not see the man's perspective.

I have realized that just because we did not work out, it did not mean he deserved to be alone and unsuccessful in his life. My ex-husband is still the father of my children, and we did share some special times together. It would only cripple me emotionally to remain in a state of loathing and hate. He was living inside of his own hell just like I was.

Imagine a man always trying to be someone other than himself because he is married to you. Think how hard it is to live a constant lie in order to keep someone in your life. A relationship can never work if one or both parties are not real about their realities. The only relationship for me worth having is one of fluid and ample communication and being able to be fearless of ridicule and reprimand from my partner.

My ex-husband made me feel I could not be who I truly was, and he must have felt the exact same way. In most situations, relationships are reciprocal. What you are receiving is what you are giving. There were some areas in my marriage where this was not true, but then there were many other areas where this did occur.

So you see, ladies, that loss was a growth for me. I realized I deserve to be loved for who I am. *We all do.* Be strong and love yourself thoroughly so you will know when the right man has come. He will fit you and your lifestyle like a glove. Do not make the mistake of holding onto the propaganda of society telling us he must be this tall, this wealthy, this handsome, this funny, and this good in bed in order to be your ideal man.

Stop selling yourself short and enjoy dating. Be open to the multitude of men and possibilities of men out there. You never know: your ideal man could be a man ten years younger, a different race than yours, a man with children already, or even a man who is right now celibate. Just try to be as open *as possible*. I still believe there is someone for everyone: we just have to be open to the possibilities. He should be whatever it is you need to complete the intimate circle only the two of you can dwell in.

Once you have found this man and have relaxed a little, hopefully you are capable of enjoying this peaceful union and restful place in your life. One of the thoughts I keep in the corners of my mind is that love should bring peace. If I do not feel peaceful, I first check myself; next I investigate the people who are around me and in my life daily.

This is a routine I consistently keep intact. It is amazing how once you have become at peace and cool within your own skin from all of the work you and you alone have done, the moment it is disturbed, an alarm inside of you goes off. My alarm doesn't just go off—it screams, "Intruder, Intruder, Intruder!"

I fight tooth and nail for my peace. If any of you reading this are Christians or have read the New Testament, one thing Christ continually says is, "I leave you in peace." Peace to me is a place where growth, love, appreciation, stillness, and power are obtained.

I try very hard not to interact with others who disturb my peace. To me, without peace you are not really living. You are existing, but also faking at life. There have been times when I get ahead of myself and have worries and pity parties because things are just not going smoothly. However, I have another way of checking myself in this situation as well. The next example will illustrate exactly how I keep myself at peace when intruders are trying to steal my joy.

There once was a young vibrant woman. She had seen many things in her life, but she had no idea what was dreadfully in store for her. The life she had created for herself was full of many milestones: she had served in the military, married, had a child, and sadly enough divorced. There were some disappointments from this life and at times she was not as fulfilled as she had hoped, but she was at least at peace with her current situation.

Shortly after her thirtieth birthday, she found out from her yearly physical that she had stage two breast cancer. Being the fighter and positive woman she was, she began the good fight—the fight for her life. She researched and applied all the knowledge she could in her life from all areas of healing, religion, proper nutrition, relaxation, herbal medicines, and perfecting an unrelenting positive spirit. Now this fight was one that took seven years of her life to complete.

All of her friends and family painfully watched how she slugged it out with the "big C." If anybody wanted to live to be an old experienced woman in this journey we call life, it was her. She was often heard by others saying, "I am going through this for a reason, but I am going to win and live to help others when they are going through difficult times in their lives." In the end, however, she let go of this fight and allowed herself the only true peace that was left for her, and that was to leave this world and go on to be with her creator, who she believed to be Jesus Christ.

Now I know firsthand how this battle may appear to have defeated this woman. This woman is my best friend, and almost every day I rely, remember, and often call on Tosha's experience to keep me focused and on point in my life when things seem to be hard, harsh, difficult, and unfair. I think about her passion to live, the obstacles she faced, and the yearning of my friend to grow old. My friend was right when she said she would be around to help others through their troubles; she just had no idea how she would do it.

I hope through the memory of her spirit I may be able to live the absolute best life I deserve and am blessed with having. Ladies, we have one shot at this thing. Please utilize it to your fullest and constantly perfect whatever is left to be perfected. There is no dress rehearsal in living; there is only one show, and it will go on with or without you. So, please, embrace this gift, love this gift, and protect this gift at all costs.

Remember when you are struggling to live, love, and be at peace with yourself, how very short life is. Remember that life is a gift and it is to be relished and rejoiced in each and every day. When life becomes difficult again, remember how equipped you are to now handle whatever comes your way. You now possess the tools of your unknown woman within; you are powerful, full of strength, able to forgive, with knowledge and wisdom to be a success at anything. My dear friends, life is not promised to any of us, so once you have found this unbelievable woman within, fight for her to the very end.

Much love and always peace,
Your friend,
Torre

A Note from the Author

Writing this book has taken me on an awesome journey of self discovery. I hope and pray whoever reads this book will become fearless in the process of self love and empowerment. It has been my pleasure sharing my life and some of my life lessons with you. May God bless and keep you forever in his grace and mercy.

Amen